WHAT RE

"TRULY ENLIGHTENING," DAVE BERNARD

"With chapters focused on topics such as "The Always There Husband" and "The Never Listens Husband," Hall addresses the realities that face many shifting to a full-time relationship. But do not despair - the author then offers suggestions to keep the relationship alive including focusing on the positive and rekindling the love that first brought you together. I particularly relate to her description of our "spousal right" to have time together as well as time apart. We all need time to do our own thing even when we are retired together, perhaps even more so."

Dave Bernard, *US News and World Report*

Nora Hall's, *Surviving Your Husband's Retirement* should be required reading for couples near or already in retirement. With real life situations and heartfelt experiences, she empowers couples to make the most of their life together in retirement. Don't try to figure out your husband or retirement on your own… or waste the first few years learning things the hard way. Let Nora's nurturing and engaging style be your guide to a successful transition together!

Robert Laura, Forbes.com contributor, retirement expert, author of *Naked Retirement*

"I felt lost because I could find no road maps for this major life transition—or even acknowledgment that it IS a major life transition. When I read *Survive Your Husband's Retirement*, I learned that other women felt the same and felt immediate relief."

Anne Cahill, Wife with a Retired Husband.

"I liked that the book was written in a light, comedic tone. That helped me not take it all so seriously—and better understand my husband's concerns."

Betsy Reece, Wife with a Semi-Retired Husband

"Insightful, practical guide to help couples survive retirement and stay married,"

Stacy Corrigan, *Manifest Your Man, Unlock the Secret to Bring Love into Your Life*

ॐ

"Sage advice, practical tools and a lot of good laughs in this humorous, compassionate, wise and spot-on book by Nora Hall."

Lisa Tener, Book Coach, Author

SURVIVE

YOUR HUSBAND'S RETIREMENT
SECOND EDITION

TIPS ON STAYING HAPPILY MARRIED IN RETIREMENT

NORA R. HALL

PUBLISHER'S INFORMATION

Author's website: www.surviveyourhusbandsretirement.com

Author contact: nora@surviveyourhusbandsretirement.com

Cover Design: Martha Langer

Font Design: Martha Rhodes

Cartoons by Randy Glasbergen

Publishing and Distribution: EBookBakery

ISBN 978-1-938517-59-4

This book is available as an ebook.

© 2017 by Nora R. Hall

In-Publication Data

Names: Hall, Nora R. (Nora Reilly), 1944-
| Glasbergen, Randy, illustrator.

Title: *Survive Your Husband's Retirement* : tips for staying happily married
in retirement / Nora R. Hall ; cartoons by Randy Glasbergen.

Description: Second edition. | [North Kingstown, Rhode Island]:
EBook Bakery, [2016] | Includes bibliographical references.

Identifiers: ISBN 978-1-938517-59-4 (softcover) | ISBN 978-1-938517-
61-7 (Kindle) | ISBN 978-1-938517-62-4 (ePub)

Subjects: LCSH: Retirement. | Older couples. | Marriage.

Classification: LCC HQ1062 .H35 2016 (print) | LCC HQ1062 (ebook)
| DDC 306.3/8--dc23

GREETINGS

When a husband retires, a wife often takes on another full-time job, but the content of this book provides many ideas to help you create a joyful retirement marriage. Workshops on bringing harmony back into your home are also available. Scan the QR code below to go to Survive Your Husbands' Retirement and find a workshop that's right for you:

Sometimes retirement is challenging, but it also offers opportunities to develop a richer relationship with your mate than you might imagine. It just takes, time, patience and compromise!

ENJOY YOUR JOURNEY.

*"Remember happiness doesn't depend upon
who you are or what you have;
it depends solely on what you think."*
–Dale Carnegie

DEDICATION

For Art

*"NOW, the best retired husband
a wife could have."*

TABLE OF CONTENTS

TELL ME THIS ISN'T HAPPENING

AN INTRODUCTION TO A HUSBAND'S RETIREMENT

"I need a better word processor for my husband.
One that will correct his spelling, grammar
and opinions."

One of my early retirement surprises came the day my ever-loving husband peeked over my shoulder and informed me how to load the washing machine. "My mother," he said, "put the clothes in one by one so she could spread them evenly and balance the load.

Unfortunately, her much too early and untimely death prevented me from knowing my mother-in-law, but I've heard stories about her that make me think we would have been great friends. However, at that moment, as I stood there quietly stuffing muddy jeans and other hiking clothes into the washing machine I couldn't decide if I wanted to whack her son with a wet sock, offer a blood curdling scream into his ear or starch his underwear. I'm certain she would have enjoyed the last option.

Our marriage wasn't always like this. We actually got along most of the time and even had fun together. But what I learned during the first months of my husband's constant presence in our home

1

is that, regardless of the state of your relationship, adjusting to retirement can be hell. For me, his changed behavior reminded me of watching the movie Terminator when Arnold Schwarzenegger transformed his human machine system into a terrifying weapon. I had expected some change when Art, my husband of 42 years, retired. Still I hadn't anticipated anything like what occurred, and I suspect he was equally surprised. I don't think either of us ever thought about the possible stress of living together day in and day out. I had dreamed of glorious days and nights in this cozy new stage of our life now that he would be released from the stress of work. After so many years of his traveling, I found myself eager for him to be home more often. I imagined candlelit dinners every evening–with him cooking occasionally–long walks on the beach whenever we wanted, and spur of the moment adventures. Perhaps we'd find a community project to work on together with double energy producing double results.

I also delighted in the possibility of my husband being here to shovel when our front walk became a winter wonderland of cold, icy, wet snow. Truth be told, the thought of turning over the electric snow blower he so kindly gave me one year for Christmas made me giddy.

Sadly, none of this happened. We didn't even get much snow for him to shovel that year. It was as if our (or at least my) retirement dreams had disappeared before they had time to begin. We squabbled like two year olds, temper tantrums and all. I sometimes felt that, when our boat for bliss blew widely off course, we boarded the one for distress and misery, suitably decorated with angry scowls and pins and needles in place of comfortable seats.

It became apparent, at least to the female on the team, that we needed to talk. The only problem was we weren't chatting very much.

Don't get me wrong; I liked this guy, and life had been good. But our track to bliss looked sadly broken. We had enjoyed shared interests while raising two great kids. Now their six children gave us ample opportunity to grandparent and spoil them, sending them home on sugar highs. So, I kept asking myself, why was I so miserable?

Not long before that day the love of my life offered his wisdom on the intricacies of loading the washing machine, I had read an AARP magazine article discussing the substantial increase in divorce when one partner retires. There were times I felt we could be the next statistic. Still, it seemed hard to fathom why couples who had somehow survived the nebulous joys of raising children, building careers, moving, settling in new neighborhoods, making ends meet, going on emergency hospital runs, paying bills, and all the other normal joys of married life, would divorce so late in the game. They had already been through the hard stuff–hadn't they? But so had we, and we weren't making life easy on one another.

"Where are we going?" I wondered. "These are supposed to be the golden years–aren't they?"

Those of us who have children know that raising kids is no picnic. I think the people who remember it as the best time of their lives have conveniently forgotten those sleepless nights with a colicky baby–or the *thrill* of waiting for your teenager to come home safely. Sure, the memories of those years sing in your heart, but, honestly, were they painless? Did they always go as planned? And, moving...when was that fun? Okay, a new house or apartment or a different area to live can be exciting, but easy? No! Given all those experiences, shouldn't retirement be a walk in the park? Why, then, did it seem so hard, and why did it hurt so?

Some days I thought about running away, far, far away, at least for a while. Maybe some space would help each of us adjust to this new life. But, divorce? That seemed pretty final–and I heard it can really screw up your retirement fund. Besides this was our problem, not just mine or his, and I knew we had to face it together. Still, I wondered how long it would be before I lost my mind. I started picturing myself as the lady in the corner pulling her hair out, strand by strand, as I speculated just how many more times he was going to ask me what time I would return from a meeting or who I was calling. It would have been so much easier had I known that all of this is a common occurrence for many newly retired couples. But I didn't. I thought I was the only person to experience these retirement troubles.

This Wasn't What I Imagined

Our retirement journey began on an ordinary day in May. When my husband left for work that morning, I anticipated him coming home weary, with more bad news, but hopeful that the company would survive a recent economic downturn. His company supplied the textile industry with materials for their manufacturing process.

Overall, the business climate for the New England textile industry faced numerous obstacles as manufacturing companies moved their factories to the south or abroad. Those who make their living in this industry know—all too well—the domino effect of New England mills and factories disappearing on a regular basis. Beautiful brick mill buildings along many rivers, now renovated for art studios or stores, serve as a testimony to historic preservation and reuse, but they also represent lost jobs and significant life changes for thousands of workers throughout the region.

Despite the obvious decline in the textile industry, I, the cockeyed optimist in the family, kept telling myself that everything would right itself. The economy would get strong quickly, the New England textile industry would revive, elephants would fly, and the world would be rosy again.

No wonder I was completely unprepared for what happened that night.

As I stood by the stove sautéing flounder for dinner, Art came to my side. He doesn't usually do that because I'm like a mother tigress protecting her den. I've been accused of growling as I physically moved a trespasser out of my sacred triangle surrounding the sink, stove, and refrigerator.

Though I normally would have read Art the riot act for infringing on my culinary territory, something in his eyes kept me from mentioning the transgression. Instead, I just looked at him.

"We're closing the company," he said. "We can't get a loan to get us through this lousy economy, and we can't make it through the slow season without a loan."

The fish sizzled in the pan as tears came to my eyes. I did not want to believe it. I couldn't believe it.

My heart shattered as I watched his sad eyes. He had worked hard to build this company and create an atmosphere of trust and respect. I grieved for my husband and for the other employees who had given their all to make the company successful.

Art had talked about retiring, but not soon and not like this, not in this rotten economy that brought pain to innocent people while others got rich. I wanted to scream, gesturing with both hands like my Italian great-grandmother used to do. But what would have been the point? It would have just given me a sore throat for the next two weeks and reduced my ability to scream about things I actually thought I could change.

Coming back to reality and realizing I had burned the fish, I heard my husband say, "We'll run the foreign operations, but we're closing the US plant, and I'm retiring in June."

"You're WHAT?!" I thought.

Talk about an earthquake. Certainly it pales in comparison to reality, but for that moment when my husband announced his retirement, I felt as if a Tsunami had picked me up and spit me out the other end. At the time, I didn't realize that this was also a foreshadowing of the unease we both would feel as we adjusted to his retirement.

After Art retired that June, we attempted to settle into this retirement marriage, but our consideration and kindness for one another disappeared like melting ice in the tropics. The only advantage to our behavior today is that we can look back on it and appreciate what we've learned–and where we never want to go again.

Retiring–whether you enjoy work or not–is hard, but when it comes earlier than anticipated, it can be downright miserable. You know that joyous expectation you have when you're getting ready for a long awaited vacation? All that disappears when you lose the opportunity to dream about how to spend your retired days and the fabulous things you would do with extra time. When retirement is thrust upon you, you may find yourself clutching your stomach and licking your wounds. That's exactly what happened to us.

"I can't believe he's retiring.
My life will never be the same."
–Wife with a Retired Husband

A Different Life Style

At the time of Art's retirement, I lived a pretty independent life. Working out of our home as a free-lance writer for small companies, I was in command of how I spent my time. I balanced work, household chores, and community involvement with time for friends and grandkids. I had planned to continue working after his retirement, but the sudden invasion of my time that Art's presence caused– even when he did nothing wrong–stunned me.

As president of a company, my husband was used to getting answers when he needed them. I, unfortunately, was not used to giving answers when he wanted them. As an independent writer, I required long periods of uninterrupted quiet time to reflect on the content at hand. He couldn't make sense of my annoyance when he innocently, bless his heart, walked into my space and started talking. I couldn't understand why he didn't see that I was in the middle of inspired, prize-winning writing or that he was stunting my creativity.

Sparks flew. I typically took audible breaths and grumbled loudly as steam shot out of my ears. He stood there, shaking his head, astonished by my response. Despite all this absurdity, I never did retrieve those perfect thoughts–nor did I win an Award for the World's Best Work in Advertising and Marketing Effectiveness, but that's beside the point. No, we just simply managed to continue to annoy one another.

Another area of our discontent also stemmed from Art's role as a company president. As much as he empowered people to do their jobs well, the buck stopped with him. He was used to making decisions and being the person in charge. Now he had only one person to be in charge of, and she did not respond so well because she thought she was in charge of herself.

When the Going Gets Tough, the Tough Get Googling

I used to hate it when my father would say, "When the going gets tough, the tough get going" in an effort to inspire me to do something. Now in my sixties, I still hate that expression but I knew it was time, once again, to act on his wisdom. I wrote in a journal when Art and I first started having what we called differences of opinion. It helped me vent, but it wasn't enough. I began scouring

the Internet, visiting book stores and searching for magazine articles in our local library that could help me understand what was
happening to our relationship in this new stage of our marriage.
True, there were plenty of books and articles on retirement, but
their topics primarily included financial security, nursing homes,
extended health care insurance, healthy life styles, and places to
live. There's no denying that all of these factors play an important
role in a happy, healthy retirement, but these weren't my concern
at the moment. I wanted to learn *how* to live with retirement–not
where to live.

I never did find any information that helped. Needless to say,
that didn't sooth my frazzled nerves.

Note: The "in charge" symptom is not unique to
company presidents. Most anyone who had even one
employee report to him, struggles in retirement with
being the person who should make the decisions and
know the answers.

Women Helping Women

Despite, or maybe because of, my frazzled nerves, I began
sharing my concerns and questions with other wives of retired
husbands, for I knew that women's ability to help one another
simply by sharing and listening can be extraordinarily effective and
helpful. I was looking for some ideas, and yes, sympathy, that would
help me get through this confusing period in our relationship. I
started to think of these comrades as fellow members in some sort
of strange club. Their stories brought me comfort and a great deal
of understanding about the necessary adjustments in a retirement
marriage. They showed me that Art and I weren't falling off a cliff
and helped me learn to laugh about and deal with his newfound
foibles. My friends' stories provided understanding and ideas to
help us get our marriage back on track. And best of all, these conversations showed me I was not alone.

I spoke with dozens of women in various situations and different
economic circumstances. Their husbands had worked in education,
the arts, construction and sales as well as in factories, administration,

service jobs, engineering, computers, and almost anything else you can think of that men do to provide for their families.

Some retired couples lived happily in retirement communities and spent time playing golf, others worked full or part time. Some women had been at-home all or most of their married life and wanted to continue to enjoy their domestic tranquility and interests—unregulated by a new boss. Economically, some had few financial constraints while many expressed concerns about the size of their retirement fund. Some of the women were old hands at this retirement game while a number had just entered this stage and expressed anxiety about the future. All, however, shared interesting comments—some funny, some sad, some scary and some surprising.

I learned in conversations with friends with retired husbands that retirement is a journey into the third stage of marriage, and are the basis for the last two of the seven commandments. For our discussion let's consider Stage I of marriage as a time for exploration and discovery, when couples get to know one another and their most intimate quirks. Stage II of a marriage is a time for career and family building.[1] Stage III is time for retirement, and that brings a host of challenges and possibilities.

The women I spoke with showed me that this new adventure called retirement can be fraught with disagreement, unhappiness, and tension or it can be filled with contentment, exploration, new understanding, and sheer joy. They showed me that we all have a choice.

Achieving joy in retirement will take work, empathy, and compromises, but the choice to accomplish that state of happiness is ours for the taking.

When I saw that my new best friends had made adjustments in their retirement marriage to meet one another's needs, I began to realize that Art and I could do that too—just as we had done in the past when difficulties crossed our path. I also found that sharing with others and learning to laugh at things that were driving me crazy made this journey into retirement marriage ever so much easier.

My friends' comments revealed that the vast majority of marriages go through a retirement adjustment period, and even women who felt that their husbands were their best friends still had to make adjustments. It's hard to say whether the shock of arguing or the disappearance of your dream for blissful retirement causes these problems, but this period is generally challenging for everyone—whether you had a great relationship or struggled throughout the years. I know I felt like Alice in Wonderland traveling down the rabbit hole, never knowing what would happen next, and I just wanted this bad dream to end.

Note to the Retiree: If you think that your partner made a remark about your behavior for this book, Congratulations! Recognition is the first step to recovery. Before you go flying off the handle like a pan flung across the room, however, keep in mind that, on average, at least four people made similar comments for each situation that's discussed. Don't flatter yourself thinking that you are the only retiree who can cause such frustration.

− THREE STAGES OF MARRIAGE −

Newlyweds
Promise, ecstasy, desire to please

తొలు

Birth of Children
Joy, excitement, exhaustion

తొలు

Retirement
Freedom, fixed income, bliss potential

Why This Book

Once I saw the void in opportunities for woman to rant, rave, cry and laugh about their retirement marriage I knew I wanted to help. Admittedly, I had reservations, for, like many other women, I was not used to baring my soul or broadcasting personal issues. Though I am not a counselor or psychologist, I am a fellow traveler. I'm also a good listener who has spoken with dozens of women with retired husbands who wanted to share their stories and help other women. I began to see that, collectively, we women could help one another prepare for and overcome the many surprises of having a husband now at home, day in and day out.

My conversations with other wives of retired husbands and the information I have culled from research on changes that occur in retirement showed me that, while husbands face major changes in retirement, we, the forgotten partners, whether we are working outside the home, working from home or who have been "at home" for some time, are just as affected by these changes as our husbands.

Some might argue that adjustment to retirement is similar to adjusting to marriage in general, but subtle differences in a newly married relationship and one of twenty, thirty or forty years precipitate varied responses and needs. It's my hope that the information in this book will help you see you are not alone, and will provide ideas to help you and your husband get over the retirement hump so you can move toward a fantastic retirement marriage.

How This Book Can Help

How do you cope or respond when you come up against a difficult or surprising situation? Do you try to make everything better, do you try to ignore it, or do you strive to find steps you can take to at least ease the discomfort? *Survive Your Husband's Retirement* will show you how women with all types of personalities and in all kinds of situations, have handled the adjustments that retirement requires in a marriage. It will also provide information on possible reasons for what many wives perceive as their husband's errant behavior. This information, along with tips from the experts, our fellow travelers down Alice's dark rabbit hole, will throw you lifelines that will help to move you from just surviving your husband's retirement to thriving together as a couple.

Each chapter in Parts I and II is based on one of *The Seven Commandments of Retirement Marriage* which you will find listed at the back of the book.

Why Seven Commandments?

After talking with my new best friends, I found five primary types of transgressions of retired husbands that make wives want to tear their hair out–or their husband's if they still have any. They are discussed in Part I of this book. In addition to a commandment, each chapter offers suggestions for maintaining sanity in your husband's retirement. Reading other women's stories might spark thoughts or ideas about your own marriage.

Your thoughts, concerns and dreams matter, so you might want to start a journal where you can write your wildest ideas, most beautiful fantasies, biggest aggravations or passionate goals. No one else need see your entries, but writing and thinking about your feelings will help you determine what you need in this phase of your retirement. By the time you finish reading this book you might even want to hold those passionate goals out for all, or at least your hubby, to see.

> **Note**: If by chance I missed your most vexing example of errant behavior in a retired husband, share that at: http://www.surviveyourhusbandsretirement.com. It's a perfect place to rant. While on the web site, you might look at the workshops that help retired wives or couples make adjustments in their retirement marriage and empower you to create the retirement of your dreams.

Part II of this book will help you move from merely surviving your husband's retirement to thriving as a couple. As in Part I, chapters 6 and 7 offer ideas on how to create a positive and loving retirement relationship with one another. They provide further information on changes that occur as you enter this potentially wonderful third stage of marriage. In Parts III and IV you'll find tips for bringing out the best in each other.

Finally, you may recall the song recorded by the Byrds, Pete Seeger and many others about there being a season for every time. The verses come from Ecclesiastes 3 in the Bible, and I quote the King James Version as I share a few verses along with some helpful thoughts to apply to your retirement marriage.

> *To every thing there is a season,*
> *and a time to every purpose under the heaven.*

Neither of you may feel certain about your purpose right now as you adjust to his retirement, but rest assured, when your spouse finds his new purpose in retirement, it will feel heavenly.

A time to kill, and a time to heal;
a time to break down, and a time to build up.

You may think you're going to break down at this point, if you don't kill him first—but wisdom, patience—and lots of forbearance—will help both of you to build a satisfying retirement marriage.

A time to weep, and a time to laugh;
a time to mourn, and a time to dance.

You may feel like weeping as you mourn this change in your relationship, but it's possible to bring back the desire to laugh and (maybe) dance with your husband again.

A time to love, and a time to hate;
a time of war, and a time of peace.

You may sometimes feel as if you're in a state of war, but after war comes peace. Here's to peace and happiness in your retirement years.

Think of this book as a tool that will help you remember that you're not alone and you **certainly aren't crazy**.

"Alone, all alone, nobody but nobody
can make it out here alone."
– Maya Angelou, from *Alone*

Part I

Five Categories of Retired Husbands

Many men enter retirement with joy and enthusiasm for this stage of life. They are the lucky ones. For the rest, countless scenarios take place during their adjustment to retirement, but–take heart–there seems to be some consistency to the misery. After hearing dozens of stories from my friends with retired husbands about his retirement, I came to realize that most of the issues causing concern, conflict or major life adjustments for newly retired couples, fit into five categories.

Don't despair! If your husband is retired, it's quite likely to have felt at some point as if you and he are the main characters in scenes from *The Bossy Husband*, *The Always There Husband*, *The Dependent Husband*, *The Angry Husband* or *The Never Listens Husband*. Time, understanding and LOTS of determination can help you create the scene of a joyful retirement marriage that works for both of you.

COMMON BEHAVIORS OF RETIRED HUSBANDS

The following five major categories can help wives identify retired husbands by type. Proper categorization doesn't correct errant behavior, but identifying your issues is a good place to begin. While your own husband may seem predominately one of the five types, most will occasionally show attributes of men in other categories.

Which Type is Your Retired Husband?

❋ Are you living with a husband who believes he has better ways to do household chores you have done effectively for five, twenty or forty years? You're living with a ***Bossy Husband.***

❋ Are you living with a retired husband who is THERE all the time? Do you feel you might trip over him as you go through your regular routine? Does the television remote seem to have lost its off button? You may have just acquired an ***Always There Husband.***

❋ Does your retired husband always want to shop with you? Are you his primary connection to the outside world? You may have the challenge of helping him move beyond the status of ***Dependent Husband.***

❋ Does your newly retired husband suddenly "fly off the handle" for no evident reason? Does he frequently mutter under his breath or blame you for everything he thinks is wrong with the world? You may be the unwilling victim of an ***Angry Husband.***

❋ Do your husband's eyes wander when you tell a story? Does he respond ah huh even though he hasn't heard a word? It's official; you are now married to a ***Never Listens Husband.***

A retired husband is often a
wife's full time job.
- Ella Harris

CHAPTER ONE

THE BOSSY HUSBAND

For our anniversay, I'm putting in a wine cellar. I need a place to keep my emotions bottled up.

A common concern I hear from women with newly retired husbands is that they can't imagine why they suddenly have a new boss. "He's always telling me what to do," many say. "I've been managing the household for years–quite well, by the way–and now he seems to think he has better ways of doing everything." One wife told me that she would gladly let her husband do the work, but all he wants is to critique hers.

Jean's Story: My Way is the Right Way

Jean liked having Tom home once he retired. They enjoyed many activities together. The bowling league they joined was great fun and they had time to see all the movies they missed over the years, and go for long walks that sometimes end with a glorious lunch. Jean also appreciated Tom's energy for cleaning. She had always done the housework; she took pride in keeping their home spotless and comfortable but delighted in the turn of events when

Tom first began to help. Washing windows with someone else made it easier and more fun than she ever imagined, and she loved it when he lugged that heavy vacuum around. Still, she had to admit that she was not prepared for the eventual consequences. Tom turned into an ultra perfectionist in his retirement. Yes, he had always been one—he was a carpenter and his customers demanded perfection, but until retirement he directed these tendencies towards work. He took pride in doing a good job and expected his helpers to do the same. If they didn't meet Tom's standards, he sent their work back until it did. Jean admired his persistent perfectionism because their livelihood depended on his reputation, and she took pride in his status as the community's preferred carpenter.

Jean's approval of his perfectionist habits held constant until he started practicing them at home. Now, with time on his hands, he thought it his duty to check everything in the house for excellence and make sure it was done according to *his* standards. Previously he never noticed how she placed his socks in the drawer. The only thing that mattered was that that they were there when he needed them. Now, he insisted that they line up one pair behind the other in neat rows by color. Spoons, had to be stacked one on top of the other in the kitchen drawer. And shirts, had to be hung by color.

Jean tended to ignore this strange development, figuring that his perfectionism was alright with her as long as he kept it to himself. However when his *suggestions* that she do certain tasks in a particular way became constant, she bristled. "How," Jean wondered, "had he become such an expert on housework, work he did little of in the years they had been married?" While grateful for his help, she questioned, "Who put him in charge?"

At first she kidded him about his sudden tidiness, but his tendency to check how well she washed dishes or the kitchen floor irked her. If he wanted to do it himself, that would be okay, but she didn't want to be told how to do it. She had, after all, done a good job for many years. Even when the kids were at home, the house sparkled. His supervision began to erode her self confidence, and her desire to keep things nice. There were days she wished he would go back to work.

Jean began to hint that maybe Tom should go out more often or perhaps take on some small contracting jobs, anything to get out of her hair. She felt exhausted from his endless criticism and the feeling of inadequacy it created inside of her. She tried to talk to Tom about how his supervision hurt her, but every time she did so, he turned the discussion back to something she, *in his opinion*, had done incorrectly. Jean was so devastated that, for the first time in their in their thirty-five years of marriage, she considered leaving him. She loved Tom, but simply could not continue living with the anxiety she felt.

The last I spoke with Jean she was still struggling with Tom's bossiness, but they are working on it, and she is confident that it will be resolved. While not liking the behavior, Jean had read about the frequent occurrences of errant behavior in a newly retired husband and has become more understanding of his needs. On his part, Tom is now aware that his bossiness is a problem for Jean. Together, they are striving to have more open conversations about this issue and continually seek ways to end this cause of strife between them. Tom has also become involved in a city-wide program helping teenagers learn carpentry. This enables him to share his wisdom where it benefits those who could use his expertise.

Behind The Errant Behavior

Why do situations like Jean's and Tom's happen, you might wonder. How can a perfectly sane man become an at-home tyrant over night? Often, when men leave their life's work, they also leave their sense of power and purpose behind, and home becomes the most convenient place to rediscover it.

For most men, but certainly not all, their life's purpose is grounded in their role as provider.[2] If your husband has identified strongly with this role, he may suffer from a perceived loss of identity and wonder about his status and self-worth. If he views retirement as a put-down, or a loss of his primary role, he could feel vulnerable and develop an unconscious need to secure power and position. For him, home is no longer just where the hearth is; it's the spot that could offer him the opportunity to regain control over something or someone, and you just may be that someone.

The loss of power is often difficult for retired men regardless of the type of work they did, but frequently, it's even more difficult for their wives. Most people in any kind of managerial position, or even if they have just one co-worker–expect their orders and ideas to be respected and acted upon. In most cases, underlings do not question the boss's decisions–and if your husband worked alone, no one questioned his decisions. The truth is, your mate's authority has been pulled out from underneath him, and he may be having as much trouble adjusting to that ignominy as you are in having to adjust to his new-found, self-assumed supremacy around your home.

Along with a lost sense of power, retirement frequently brings a lost sense of purpose. In his book, *Men Are From Mars, Women Are From Venus,* John Grey notes that, "not to be needed is a slow death to a man."[3] With retirement, many men sense that their role as providers for their families have been scooped out from under them and may feel as if they've been thrown out with the trash as their search for a new role begins.

Spending more time at home gives retired husbands ample opportunity to examine the situation and devise ways to make things *bigger, better, faster.* Thus the rattling off of orders becomes part of some husbands' effort to continue taking care of his family. As you strive to understand the root of his errant behavior it will be helpful to consider what might be behind your husband's actions.

A third possibility for his new behavior is that he hasn't found anything better to do with all this new-found time.

If you're confronted with the problem of a husband who suddenly knows all there is to know about managing a household and wants to tell you how you've been doing things wrong all these years, you have the empathy of every wife with a retired husband. It's not an uncommon disease in the early stages of retirement. Few of us are prepared for the hurdle of adjusting to retirement and, since he's a guy, he'll probably be the last person to admit there's a problem. He may need some help in finding his way through it.

It will take time and effort to sort out the causes for his new-found behavior and how to resolve the issues. But, even after many years of marriage, we can still learn more about each other. This learning curve was an important factor for Jean and her bossy husband Tom. Jean was suffering from his apparent desire to control everything and wasn't sure how to stop it. Despite her comments he didn't realize that his frequent commands truly upset her. Some might wonder why Tom didn't read Jean's body language, but that skill is one women utilize more frequently than men. It doesn't seem to appear in the male genetic code.

Tom was truly surprised when Jean finally got him to see that his constant *suggestions* on how to do things differently presented a problem. He thought he was showing his willingness to be helpful.

"Having to suddenly deal with a bossy husband
or one who insists he's always right
is like getting mumps on your wedding day
–darn inconvenient and not much fun."
– Wife with a Bossy Husband

Your Spousal Right: Freedom From Constant Critique

Jean, like many wives, felt driven to distraction by her retired husband's comments on everything she said or did. His frequent evaluation of every thing she did made her nervous, and she frequently found herself doing stupid things she would never have done before.

You've done an excellent job of home management for many years. Sure, things can always be done differently, but why fix something that isn't broken? It's your right to expect, and demand if necessary, respect for how you have managed the household throughout the years, but you may have to point this out to your wannabe boss.

Survival Tips for Wives With Bossy Husbands

When confronted with a Bossy Husband, it could prove helpful to ask yourself how he might be feeling about the particular situation. This thought process will help you reflect on what he is experiencing in the wake of retirement and perhaps feel some empathy for his situation. Don't be surprised, however, when those insights don't completely help to anticipate his response. If you've been married for more than a month, you've likely learned that he responds quite differently to most situations than you do. Still, just being aware of possible reasons for his distress can help you develop a rational plan of attack on his newfound–and not so wondrous–behavior.

It's also quite possible that your attempts to help will not seem appreciated at first. I've never heard a scientific explanation of why men need to solve their own problems with their own solutions, but

I suspect it has much to do with the reality that boys are generally encouraged, or genetically wired, to present a strong front with solutions for every problem. There are times I see this even in my four-year-old grandson.

Your efforts to understand your husband's current struggle will help you develop tools to effectively approach the problem of his bossiness. The steps listed below will help you clarify your difficulties with his behavior, before you approach the issue with him. You might want to use a journal as you consider these steps and take the time to write your answers to some of your questions or concerns. Then in six or seven months, you will be able to look back and compare how you feel now to how you felt then and see the progress you and your husband have made.

* Decide what is important and what changes you truly need.

* Define why his display of authority bothers you.

* Identify what he did at a certain time that created a problem for you.

* Describe how it makes you feel.

* Consider how you'd like him to deal with the situation.

It's also important for you to remember that in your husband's mind there are probably several good reasons for his bossiness. It does not mean, however that you must accept the behavior. When he suggests ways to change your successful routines or your manner of doing something around the house you can:

* Insist the confirm how his way is better, smarter or faster.

* Verify why he feels it's important to make the change.

* Adopt his idea if you agree with the assessment.

* Feel no obligation to comply if you don't agree.

- ❋ Let him go for it if he wants to do the task himself in a satisfactory alternate way.
- ❋ Say that more hands getting the work done, the merrier!

Your preparation for these important discussions will help you clarify your position and feelings so you can orchestrate a calm and productive conversation–not as an opportunity for *tit for tat*. Even if you've never had a calm and productive conversation before, now is the first day of the rest of your life. Both you and your husband have needs, and it's reasonable for them to be dealt with fairly and openly.

Just one reminder: Since your husband many not be aware of your difficulty with his new retirement behavior, you'll need to initiate the conversation. As some might say...the ball is in your court!

Coping Secrets From Other Wives With Bossy Husbands

Susan, a fellow retirement traveler, developed an easy remedy for the "command syndrome" when her husband Jim acted as if he had re-joined the military and developed an army sergeant fashion of rattling off orders to their grandkids. It was irritating to all concerned, but he didn't realize the problem. She helped fix it with a little bit of humor and a gentle refusal to surrender her independence or needs. Without much discussion of the problem, Susan learned to smile and give him the "zip-your-lips" signal by running her finger across her lips. This simple action on her part helped Jim get the picture and stop spouting commands, at least for the moment. On occasion she still has to remind him with a quick zip you lips motion.

Carol made note of the types of activities her husband, Owen, seemed to want to be in charge of–or at least change how she normally performed those tasks. After a few weeks of listening to his commands she selected those that bothered her the most and showed him her list. Apparently he hadn't realized that he gave so many commands or how it was affecting her. Once he had the concrete evidence, however, he had to acknowledge how annoying his behavior could be for her. Now he continues to try to remember that he's not her boss.

"If you wonder why your husband does something that bothers you, ask him! That's ask, not accuse. Together, you just might find an answer and a solution.
– Arielle Eckstut

Chapter Two

The Always There Husband

© Randy Glasbergen
www.glasbergen.com

GLASBERGEN

"How can you say we never go anywhere together? I've been following you all day on Twitter!"

"**H**e's always there!" If you spend any time with wives of retired husbands, this is a statement you're sure to hear over and over again. No matter how much we care for our husbands, we're simply not used to them being there all the time. We're not used to the questions, to the feeling of being watched as we go through our daily activities or to the interruptions to our routines.

Kate's Story: The Kitchen Stomp

"Cooking has never been my great love," said Kate as we sat with a cup of tea and crumpets she had made, "but," she continued, "I usually managed to put out a decent meal, and when the kids were small, we always baked together."

Kate told me that she seldom, if ever, bakes now because she feels that she and her husband don't need all the calories–and she really hates to follow a recipe. Still, even with eliminating the baking she finds herself cooking and cleaning up a lot more than she cares to.

Sometimes Kate wishes that Doug would cook occasionally, but working together in their small kitchen is a problem. She also is uncomfortable with Doug's practice of sitting in the kitchen while she's cooking. She said, "It really unnerves me. I know he wants to keep me company, but sometimes I feel as if I'm taking (and failing) my final exam at the culinary arts school."

Kate described how, from his perch on the other side of the counter, Doug frequently asked her why she was doing something a certain way or exclaimed that she is going to burn the bacon with such high heat. Can't you just imagine her *thrill* at being told she wasn't cooking something correctly even though he had been eating it with delight for the past forty years? "He's never cooked the dish in his entire life. What makes him think he knows how to do it better than I do?" she wondered aloud. It was the last straw. Kate blew up and, in her frustration, demanded that Doug help with the cooking.

And so began the *kitchen stomp.*

"Why is it," Kate asked, "that two women can work in the kitchen together for hours and never step on one another's toes or hinder the other's progress? It's almost as if we choreograph our own kitchen dance, moving a hip sideways so the other can pull a knife from the holder or reach the drawer for a pan. And we do it instinctively—without a word."

"When my husband's cooking with me," Kate continued, " Everything takes me longer. I have to maneuver around him making sure that my feet don't get stepped on as he drags himself out of the way of a cabinet or the sink. The dynamics are totally different."

Kate admitted that summer is better. Her husband takes pride in his grilling skills and will cook most anything on it. She likes the fact that she does the prep and he does the cooking, but she's still trying to figure out what she'll do when winter comes again.

As we continued talking, Kate decided that she would discuss the possibility with Doug of his cooking one night a week on his own. The idea of him deciding what to cook and how to prepare it sounded marvelous to her. Best of all, this plan would enable her to stay out of the kitchen at least that one night a week.

Lisa's Story: The Transformed Engineer

"He thinks he should manage everything I do," Lisa protested when I first met her. "After twenty years of managing projects for a civil engineering company, he thinks he's the only one who can control anything...the cleaning, the shopping, my time with friends."

Lisa knew that a lot of people had depended on her husband to make certain that projects ran smoothly and were completed on time, but "he can't manage me or the way I run the household," she wailed as tears flowed down her cheeks.

Lisa had her hands full. Bob, a happy, energetic man, took early retirement even though he wasn't completely ready to give up his reign of responsibility. Whether building a foundation for a bridge or demolishing a building, his job had required him to be on top of details such as safety, permits, supplies, scheduling, and the political insanity that goes with major construction or deconstruction, such as blowing up buildings.

Lisa admitted Bob's job had been stressful and required constant attention to detail, but she said, "it couldn't have been any more traumatic for him than what he is doing to me right now. I think he'd be happy if I ran around with flashing lights going beep, beep like a truck backing up and stopping only to ask if I had gone to the right place." With clenched fists she cried, "I want to control my own life again. He has so much ability and energy. Why would he waste all of that following me around making sure I'm doing the right thing?" Lisa quipped that she sometimes imagines him with a clipboard checking off everything she does right and wrong.

Lisa had enjoyed the idea that Bob's retirement would give them more time together. She had also fantasized about his taking over some household tasks; she would gladly give up the vacuum and the grocery list if he would offer. Her dream of having more time to paint and show her work would come true, she thought, and selling a few more pieces of art each month would offset Bob's newly reduced income.

When he retired, Bob had offered to help with the housework, but it didn't quite work out according to Lisa's dream.

"He wants to do everything with me. I guess to check that I do it right. I back up from dusting the coffee table, and he's right there plumping pillows. I suspect he stays so close to check that I get every morsel of dust off the table. If he wants to help, why can't he choose a task on the other side of the room? Sometimes I think he's going to follow me into the bathroom—to make sure I'm even doing that right!"

"Plus," Lisa said, "It takes the two of us twice as long working like that."

Bob's behavior went on for about three months. Although Lisa felt that she could stand it no longer, she still did not know what to do. She didn't want to alienate him or make him feel that his presence annoyed her, nor did she want to embarrass him, but his hovering had to change.

Bob had never been a hobby person; his work and family consumed most of his pre-retirement time, and he had been content with that lifestyle. Work as a civil engineer kept him fully engaged, and even at home he read engineering material and contemplated solutions for projects. Once he gave up work, he seemed to give up his interest in engineering, but apparently not the supervision skills he had developed. Lisa felt grateful he had not given up his interest in family even if she occasionally felt that he now put too much emphasis on that aspect. She needed some space—and Bob needed some new interests to engage him and keep his mind active and happy.

Lisa started probing, hoping to help Bob identify activities he might enjoy besides supervising her. She asked him about projects he worked on before retiring; why they built the last bridge the way they did; how he decided what kind of a bridge would go in a particular place. At first, Bob gave brief answers to her questions, looking miserable as he responded. Did he fear that discussing previous projects would end his retirement—take him back to work?

This surprised Lisa because Bob had always taken pride in his work and enjoyed talking about it. She couldn't understand his response. Was he so eager to change his life, or sorry he had left the old one behind, that he felt if he talked about previous projects, he couldn't make this new life work for him? She desperately wanted to help him, but how?

About three months after Bob retired, their discussion took an interesting twist while they were window-shopping downtown. It evolved from a display of an erector set at the local toy store. Bob explained how a toy like that had developed his interest in engineering. He mentioned the spatial awareness skills that building projects require and how he became aware of that while playing with his first erector set. This intrigued Lisa. She had never heard how Bob had developed his engineering interests, and this conversation gave her an idea. She suggested they get a set for their soon-to-be 12-year-old granddaughter.

"She won't be interested," Bob said. "Kids today are only interested in electronics."

"I'll bet if you did it with her, she would love it. It would be something special for the two of you to do together. You might enjoy it, and you can show her engineering isn't just for boys," Lisa said.

Reluctantly Bob agreed, so they bought and wrapped the erector set for Marci's birthday. Although somewhat mystified when she opened it, her eyes brightened when Grandpop told her he would show her how it worked.

Bob and Marcie spent hours together enjoying one another's company and creating together. They started out with simple projects so Marcie could see how the set worked, but when they created a draw bridge that moved up and down, Marcie glowed. Her cousins thought all of this was pretty cool and seemed a little jealous. They wanted to do things like that with Grandpop.

Once Bob realized how much he enjoyed working with Marcie on her projects, he and Lisa decided that an age-appropriate erector set, along with a certain number of hours every week with Grandpop, would be wonderful birthday gifts for the other grandchildren as well. This decision brought many benefits to the entire family.

The outcome of Bob's finding something that gave him a purpose, was significant for both of them. Their marriage had been struggling from the stress of Bob's hovering, and when he wasn't trailing behind Lisa around the house, he felt lost and lethargic. Once Bob discovered something that really mattered to him, he agreed to take on responsibility for doing the household tasks he did best and enjoyed most—on his own schedule. The necessary tasks seemed to be accomplished faster and, now that Lisa no longer felt that her effectiveness as a homemaker was in question, she began to relax and enjoy life again. As a result, she went back to her favorite hobby and started painting pictures that were even more beautiful than those she had done before. The upshot–she sold three paintings in a short time.

From Bob's perspective, working with his grandchildren in this fashion was the best gift he could ever have received. This special time with each of them, a time he never took before, brought joy to Bob's life.

When the children came to the house to work with Grandpop they transformed the once quiet family room into a bustling, excited den of builders. The energy they brought into the house for their building projects ignited Lisa's and Bob's enthusiasm. His zest for life that had been missing the first few months of retirement was back.

"I just need some space; I never have the house to myself.
He even tries to follow me into the bathroom."
– Wife with an Ever Present Husband

Both Lisa and Bob are now busy doing things they each enjoy. Their sense of purpose has grown enormously, and they have new energy for joint activities that don't include housework.

Behind the Errant Behavior

From the dozens of women I have spoken with about retired husbands I've learned that women tend to be nesters much more so than men. As we observe the behavior of men and women in the 21st century, it seems reasonable to say that most women–working full time or not–take on the care of our homes as well as the bulk of housework. We just seem to have a greater need for our living space to be in order than men do. This may not be true for everyone, but if you've ever moved as a couple ask yourself, who felt more unsettled–you or your husband–until everything was put away and looked the way you felt it should? Your answer can tell you a great deal about how you relate to your home and why you're feeling that your newly retired husband is invading your space. If you're concerned that your newly retired husband's actions disrupt your nest, you're probably not pregnant (thank God for Menopause). However, our feminine makeup or the maternal instinct, typically prompts us to be more psychologically invested in keeping our homes up to certain standards.[4] While your husband may certainly appreciate your home and assume a great deal of responsibility for its upkeep and maintenance, he might not feel as protective of his space as you do. If women are *nesters* perhaps we should think of men as *lodgers*—people who are comfortable and invested in where they live, but not gravely concerned about the color of the walls.

Perhaps this is one of the reasons your husband may not understand your dismay over his sudden disruption of the environment you have so carefully created. Yes, you decorated your home for both of you, but be honest, don't you see yourself as the one in charge of that environment?

The differences in men's and women's typical emotional leanings give rise to major differences in how we (as women) perceive our surroundings versus the way our husbands perceive it. It is usually difficult for men to empathize with us on our reaction to their now almost constant presence in the home. If he's sensitive at all to your discomfort, he's probably wondering what the heck is wrong with you. He may be thinking, "I live here, too. Don't I?" or "Where else am I going to be now that I don't have an office or work to go to?" Most likely, it's difficult for him to imagine that you too are struggling with these retirement adjustments. He may be thinking "Your life hasn't changed" or "Why aren't you glad that I'm here?"

Your Spousal Right: Time Together and Time Apart

During your early years of marriage, your time together and apart from one another probably fell into place without much thought. One or both of you had jobs and, if you had children, caring for them probably filled the rest of your time. In retirement, everything changes. We've come to a state where our choices and priorities—not those of our boss or our kids—can dictate our use of time. How we spend this time in the last third of our marriage will contribute to—or take away from—the level of bliss we experience.

Whether or not you go out to work every day, your husband's retirement will require some agreements on the use of time. You're going to need to do your routine, but, if you like the fact that he's around, you may also want to restructure some of your day to enjoy your togetherness.

29

Retirement can be disconcerting for men who have spent their lives going to work and generally having the structure of their days dictated by the job. During their working years, many men came home for dinner just as it was being put on the table. And many wives planned the bulk of the social engagements. With retirement, home becomes much more than a place to sleep and eat. It can be confusing, depressing and confounding for men to figure out how to fill these new hours (and hours!) at home. Retirement can be disorientating–but that doesn't give your husband permission to hover.

Survival Tips for Wives with Retired Husbands

As often as women mention time alone in their list of concerns, most men have difficulty even imagining that their wives struggle with this issue. This could be another conversation the two of you have, but consider the following before you enter this particular retirement dance:

* Men and women typically have very different ways to approach any task.

* As nesters, women often personalize the responsibilities for their homes, but men tend to be "lodgers," who don't think as much about the color of the walls or...

* It may be difficult for your husband to imagine that you too are struggling with adjustments to his retirement.

* Once upon a time you and your husband had common interests that got set aside in the course of life.

* You might want to pull out your journal again as you prepare for this conversation.

* Be clear with yourself about what makes you feel he's hovering.

* Evaluate how you previously spent time apart. Identify what you enjoyed doing together before retirement.

- Pull out that bucket list and consider what you would like to do together now.
- Make certain that each of you has ample time to do the things you wish to do.
- Be clear about your goals for togetherness.

"Without a passionate spark, two people living together may be lonelier than living alone."
– **Helen Simpson,** *Major Pettigrew's Last Stand*

Coping Secrets From Other Women With Retired Husbands

Even though they enjoy one another's company tremendously, Sally and Mike have decided to spend at least one day a week on their own. She has the house to herself on Tuesdays and he has it on Thursdays. Their alone time enhances their enjoyment of their time together. If absence does truly make the heart grow fonder, this may be good for your relationship as well.

Mary Anne and her husband, Steve, designate one day a week a *Date Day* to do something special together. The beauty of their plan is that they know there is time they will spend together, but they don't have to spend every moment in one another's company. What they choose to do on these dates runs the gamut of activities–but no errands. Together they evaluated their *bucket lists* and discovered affordable interests that add spark to their retirement marriage.

BJ and Bill decided they liked the *Date Day* idea, but they added an interesting twist. Every week one of them is responsible for planning a Mystery Trip. This has caused fun competition between them and has taken them to places or to experience activities that they never would have even considered before.

Kate and Doug in the *Kitchen Stomp* story could consider taking cooking lessons together. Classes might help them learn to use their kitchen space–together or separately–or even help Doug feel better about taking on the cooking one night a week by himself.

"If you want to change your life, you have to think differently."
– **Andy Andrews**

CHAPTER THREE

THE DEPENDENT HUSBAND

Sometimes when a husband retires, he tends to depend on his wife for his social life–often wanting to accompany her wherever she goes because he hasn't yet figured out what else to do with himself.

Rachel's Story: Finding the Right Sock Drawer

Roger's and Rachel's vacation home in San Diego was their Shangri La. It provided relief from the winter cold for Rachel and a place to relax for Roger. Three bedrooms offered plenty of space for them and for their guests who always enjoyed their hospitality and the spacious outdoor environment their vacation home offered. However, when they decided to make this house their permanent residence, the challenge of making it feel like *home* began.

It made sense for them to move; cold weather tortured Rachel, and Roger enjoyed playing golf year round. There couldn't be a better place for them. The mortgage was paid, and they had decorated it their way when they bought it three years before. The house had a garden, but not too much, and it was part of a built in community where "displaced" northerners were eager to meet new friends. Still the strains of home tugged at their hearts.

In many ways Rachel adjusted more easily than Roger. Nonetheless she still pined for things familiar from her home up north. She found herself seeking that warm fuzzy feeling that comes to mind when we think of home and wondered how she would replace all the wonderful memories or the smell of a wood fire on a cold evening. Easy access to family and old friends also worried her, but the pleasant experiences during the winters she spent in San Diego before her husband retired, assured her that this was a good move.

Roger had more difficulty. Although he said he had retired, his life and mind-set were still up north. He had been a successful marketing consultant when he decided to slow down. He kept two long-term clients and agreed to stay with them for two years while helping them find a good match for his replacement. With the need to travel north at least one week a month, Roger never felt really *at home* in his new home. He also kept the companies' records in the guest room of their *retirement* home.

Roger, previously a meticulously neat individual, started leaving his stuff everywhere once he moved in. So now, in addition to his feelings of edginess and of being at loose ends much of the time, Rachel needed to deal with his being a pack rat. Why he needed four computers in their small home was beyond Rachel's understanding. Deciding where to put things or how to arrange his new life morphed into an all-consuming process for Roger. He felt off kilter with not having a convenient place for his belongings and not knowing what to do with all the stuff he had brought with him. Roger once told Rachel that if he could just find the right sock drawer three days in a row he'd be all set.

At first Rachel tolerated the mess, figuring it would eventually get straightened out. But when his edginess manifested itself in questioning her everyday activities and asking her to account for everything she did, her living situation became intolerable.

Roger had enjoyed coming down every other week when Rachel spent the winter in San Diego. Their new friends in their southern home, however, were mostly hers and people she had come to know during her extended stays. Unfortunately Roger felt like a visitor devoid of his own activities and wanted to spend all of his time with Rachel. He even wanted to go to the grocery store with her.

Shopping together wouldn't have been a problem if, like Rachel, Roger enjoyed meandering into several stores just looking to see what was new. Unfortunately he was a make your list and get in and get out kind of person.

"Where are you rushing to?" Rachel would ask, but a statement like that reminded him he didn't have a place to rush to. She begged him to slow down, to relax and enjoy every moment, or at least find his own activities before he drove her crazy.

Roger wanted to oblige Rachel, but he couldn't turn a switch and make it all happen. He looked forward to warmth in the winter and a more relaxed lifestyle, but he missed the comfort and familiarity of their home up north.

Eventually Roger volunteered at a local school and signed up to play golf two mornings a week. Rachel thought she had a solution. At least it brought some relief. Free of the need to answer his questions, "Why are you going there? Why does it take so long to pick up a few things at the store? Why did you go that way?" she could now wander in stores or walk through the park on her own whim. This pleased Rachel. She felt they had reached a reasonable compromise.

Martha's Story: I Don't Want To Be His Social Director

"I have my job, and that didn't change when he retired, but he wants to go all these places, and do all kinds of new things together. Some of it is good, but dinner still has to be cooked, clothes still have to be washed, and the house needs to be cleaned. How can I do all of that if we take off all the time?" Martha said when we talked.

Martha's sleepless nights were taking their toll, but she could not decide what to do. She could quit her job, but that idea didn't please her. She loved working at the school as a part time tutor; it kept her stimulated and alert. Martha felt part of the community and in touch with what students were thinking and doing. She also felt that she had a great deal to offer—especially to those students who might flunk if it weren't for the extra help she gave them. She knew how much the kids' parents appreciated her efforts. Martha simply couldn't give up this job that meant so much to her. *And* that meant something had to change at home.

Dan could not understand what was happening to them—why Martha seemed to resent the time he wanted to spend with her. "I'm retired," he said. "We finally have more time together. Don't you remember how you always wanted to go for walks and share ideas? Now you tell me you don't have time? What gives?" he asked. "Why are you so cranky?"

Martha didn't mean to be cranky. She enjoyed Dan's company and wanted to spend more time with him, just not all of the time. Before Dan retired Martha had a routine, up early to get a few household tasks done before leaving for school, run errands or visit with friends on her way home, then relax with Dan in the evening. She didn't work on Friday so she always used that time to finish her housework and get caught up on whatever else needed to be done. Now Dan expected her to plan an outing for every Friday.

Martha liked the concept of a new activity each week, but wondered why Dan couldn't plan it at least sometimes.

"You're the teacher," he often replied. "You're supposed to know all the interesting places around here. You've always talked about how people learn through hands-on experiences. I would think you could come up with ideas."

"But I wasn't hired to be your social director. You do the planning, and I'll dance with you," she told him.

Eventually Dan recognized that, although Martha wanted to do things with him, she needed his help to plan the outings. His efforts to respond to her needs resulted in some interesting outcomes that are discussed later in this chapter.

Behind the Errant Behavior

When husbands find themselves without the demands of work, they may feel lonely or wonder what to do with this new-found time. Who do they turn to when they're down? You, of course! His presence can be a welcomed experience, but it's not fun if he trails behind you all day and wants to know the why and what of everything you do.

Time and new discoveries will likely resolve some of your husband's angst, but in the meantime, you'll want to take steps to maintain your sanity. You may need to practice patience and be understanding of his situation, but you have rights also. Because Dan saw that he had much to gain by agreeing to Martha's ultimatum, their transition from dependence to independence was relatively easy. Yours might seem more difficult to you at the moment, but don't give up on your right to insist on a resolution that works for both of you.

Like most negotiations, the more you make it a win-win situation for each of you, the more success you'll have in getting your husband to understand that his lack of energy or increased dependence on you is stressful for you and your relationship.

Your Spousal Right: Respect for Your Routine

Whether you work outside the home, work from home or are the full-time manager of your home, you no doubt have a comfortable and productive routine. You probably do your daily household tasks or prepare to leave for work without much thought. Suddenly your husband is there, and maybe you can't take a shower at your usual time or make the bed when you get up. Sounds simple—or maybe petty—but these things cause friction that may lead to arguments about something totally unrelated.

In the chapter on The Always There Husband I referenced our tendency as women to be "*nesters*". That makes us more sensitive to the changes happening in our household management procedures. Although your husband could be totally unaware of your feelings, you have the right and the responsibility to be heard about your difficulty. You don't need to nag or be a shrew, but it will be beneficial for both of you to speak up about your concerns.

I know I had to admit to my husband's accuracy about this when, a decade or two ago, he informed me he couldn't change something if he didn't know what the problem was or even that there was a problem. Until then I expected him to simply understand I had an issue with something, but honestly how could he have known what caused steam to come out of my ears if I didn't tell him?

In Martha's story Dan was surprised and resistant when she told him he must plan the excursions if he wanted to explore new places together. He was equally as surprised when she told him she needed help around the house if they were going to have more time for fun.

Once Dan got over his resistance to being the planner and started looking for places to visit, he learned a great deal about his home state. The research renewed his interest in history and inspired him to become active with his community's Historic Preservation Committee.

For most, retirement becomes more meaningful when we pursue interests that energize us. Martha's insistence that Dan take responsibility for planning their weekly outing led him to discover new interests that renewed his zest for life.

Survival Tips for Wives with a Dependent Husband

The more retired men have a network of friends and engaging activities, the more likely they are to achieve a happy retirement. Sadly some couples worry that a fixed retirement income makes it risky to take on new activities that may become expensive. However, discussing ideas can help you develop an affordable plan. Consider the following statements because helping your husband establish a plan can hasten his transition into a delightful retirement.

* When first retiring, men may feel disengaged from life.

* Husbands who find meaning in retirement life are less likely to look to their wives as their primary connection to the outside world.

* Each spouse has a need for his or her own space, interests and routines.

* Agreement on the use of time and space is a matter of understanding one another's needs.

* Part of the problem may be your or your husband's perception of the problem.

* Meaningful activities spark enthusiasm and make everyone happier.

Coping Secrets from Other Wives

When John first retired he went on an austerity kick, feeling that he had to make sure they had enough money for the rest of their lives. His wife, Tina, was sympathetic to his concern until she realized he was quickly loosing his zest for life and his health as well. All day long he sat reading a newspaper or watching TV because he thought they were inexpensive activities to fill his days. When nagging to get him moving did nothing, Tina started tallying up the costs he was incurring through these *inexpensive* activities. She noticed that their electrical costs went up from the increased TV usage and that the food bill was billowing just like his waist line. Even though John seldom wore anything but old sweat pants, he was going to need larger clothes soon if he didn't stop snacking so she calculated those costs as well.

Next Tina began to estimate how much more they would incur in medical bills since he became a couch potato. Her written report on his supposed frugal expenses showed John that he wasn't being quite as thrifty as he had thought. He realized he could actually afford—and would benefit from—at least one new activity that would interest him and bring back his enthusiasm for life. He even agreed to "break the bank" and have the broken tire on his bike fixed so that he could ride it every day.

*"His spirit of creativity and exploration
went out the window with the paycheck"*
– Wife with a Dependent Husband

CHAPTER FOUR

THE ANGRY HUSBAND

If I smile, the rest of my body will think I'm in a good mood. And then my feet will want to go out dancing. And then I might meet another woman on the dance floor. And then I might have to pay you alimony. That's why I never smile."

Anger is not a pretty thing, and when it feels directed at you 24 hours, 7 days a week it becomes a problem for your health and sanity. It's a crucial issue that must be addressed as soon as possible and may need outside guidance.

Stacey's Story: You're Retired, Not in Kindergarten

"Damn! What's his problem now?" Stacey moaned. Bill's moods disturbed her. Generally an upbeat and happy person, Bill had morphed into a sullen fuss-budget. The hardest part was that predicting those moods had become impossible. For no apparent reason, at least that Stacey could see, he would start sputtering about something that annoyed him.

Stacey hated confrontation; most of their married life she tried to create a happy, comfortable atmosphere for both of them. For the most part it had worked, but now that she found herself needing to be the pacifier day in and day out, her ideas for managing their happiness and her energy quickly disappeared. Resentment took over.

"He decided to retire," she said, "and it is not my fault that he now uses his extra time to find problems everywhere." She understood that these were his issues, but she didn't like being the brunt of his outbursts.

For the most part Stacey tried to be kind to Bill. When his anger took hold she'd take a deep breath and either walk away or simply tell him she didn't like what he was doing. She also tried to compliment him on the good things he did when he wasn't being angry.

After a few weeks of Bill's childish tantrums however, Stacey lost patience. Despite her dislike of confrontation she demanded some action. "You get annoyed over the simplest events or some side remark you happen to overhear. It's tiresome and it needs to stop," she insisted. Bill took offense at this as well, but Stacey resolved to end this household misery and continued to call him on every outburst. He groused or sulked for several weeks, but she persisted because she wanted to end this wretched state of affairs caused by his anger.

After weeks of her insistence that Bill change his ways, Stacey threatened to leave before he sent her to the hospital. Many times Bill had heard Stacey tell him that his outbursts put her in a bad mood, and that she was tired of his behavior, but that day he finally heard the anxiety in her voice and realized that he needed to change his behavior. Something in her tone made him think maybe he owned the problem.

Previously when Stacey complained about his moodiness he would reply that he didn't know why he felt irritated all the time but never offered any solutions. This day, however, he realized that he really didn't want to hurt Stacy. He thought about her kindness and patience and realized that he, and he alone, needed to make the change. For the first time since his retirement, he told Stacey he would work on his anger and do his best to change. Stacey told him that she would hold him to that promise.

Bill had worked for a heating company since he graduated from technical school and, for ten years before retiring, had been responsible for overseeing the installation of air conditioners in private homes. Now he had nothing to be in charge of except himself. Stacey's outburst that morning made him realize he wasn't succeeding at his new job.

Bill began to take a serious look at his new retirement behavior. It occurred to him that when something went wrong at work, he had asked why and found a solution to the problem. Now, he just got annoyed and allowed himself to feel miserable—mostly over things that didn't matter. The realization that *he* was the problem gave him a start, but it also gave him a mission. When he acknowledged the issue, life became better for both Bill and Stacy. The problem wasn't solved immediately, but his awareness of the issue made it possible for him to look for solutions.

The last time Stacey and I spoke, she was still waiting to see the end of all his outbursts but was delighted that they occurred much less frequently now. When they do, Bill tries to catch himself quickly. Stacey appreciates that Bill is doing everything he can to change his behavior because he recognizes the pain his anger causes her.

"He gets angry at the simplest things.
I don't understand it; he never did that before."
– Wife of an Angry Husband

Behind the Errant Behavior

Don't be surprised, if your husband is discouraged, lost or disappointed because he's retired or if he develops a tendency to become angry over simple things. Scientists at the Mayo Clinic state that our attitudes are the result of an organized collection of thoughts, and these thoughts dictate much of our behavior. It could be that your husband's disappointment in retirement leads him to act in an angry manner because he has created an organized collection of negative thoughts that prompt him to think negatively about almost everything. The key to moving from anger is to eliminate the negative thinking patterns scientists call filtering, personalizing, catastrophizing or polarizing. Any of these negative thinking patterns can lead people to all sorts of strange behavior. For instance, when our mind is *Filtering* information we tend to eliminate all the encouraging aspects of any situation. When we *Personalize* a situation, we blame ourselves every time something bad happens. When we *Catastrophize*, we expect the worst possible outcome in any situation, and when we *Polarize*, we see failure as anything short of absolute perfection.[5] Who wouldn't be angry when stuck in any of these situations? Goodness, it sounds as if it is time to help him move away from all of this!

Another source of a retired husband's anger could be a condition called andropause. Studies indicate that this medical condition brings about a decrease in testosterone in older men. It affects their quality of life and may spark grumpiness. Although the first study of this condition was published in the Journal of the American Medical Association in the mid-1940s, not a great deal of research has been conducted because, not surprisingly, many men refuse to discuss the issue. Based on limited studies, it is believed that balancing hormones may help relieve the situation.[6]

Physicians do connect some grouchiness to the hormone decrease in andropause, but there is no clear evidence that supports a particular medical treatment for all grumpy old men. However, it may help you to be a bit more understanding if you know that there might be a physical cause (and remedy) to your husband's grumpiness. That doesn't mean you have to accept the behavior; it just means you might want to insist that your husband has a discussion with his doctor about his behavior. If it's not investigated as a possibility, you'll never know if there could be a solution.

If there is no medical reason for his anger or grumpiness, then it will be necessary for you to take other steps. Talking with other women with retired husbands may help you get a better sense of the cause of his anger and reveal some solutions for your situation. Depending on its severity, you may also want to encourage him to seek psychological counseling for him or for you as a couple if you feel that would be more effective. Regardless of what you decide to do, it's important to remember IT'S NOT YOUR FAULT.

Finally, your husband could be grumpy simply because, as we've discussed before, he's angry that he is retired or confused about how to spend his days. This feeling of a lack of purpose comes up time and time again for many retirees so, once again, we need to challenge our retired husbands to develop a plan for successfully channeling their energy and interests.

Your Spousal Right: Respect for Your Happiness, Health and Feelings

Living with a grouchy or angry person often causes stress and depression and is hazardous to your health. Whatever the cause of your husband's anger it is important for you to remember that it's his problem. He, not you, must fix it and build a retirement life that has meaning for him.

You are not to blame for his contentious approach to life. However, a positive and take-charge attitude could become contagious. Strong insistence on his civil behavior will likely prompt him to consider taking the necessary steps that will move him out of the hole of hopelessness he's stuck in.

Survival Tips for Wives with an Angry Husband

Dealing with an angry husband is potentially the most difficult situation any wife can face. Not only is it miserable living in an argumentative environment, but it's often difficult to reason with an angry person. For your own health and sanity, you must speak out against such behavior, clearly and often. You will both suffer if your husband's anger becomes habit, so you'll want to consider the following thoughts.

❖ The more a person expresses anger, the more that anger becomes habitual.

❖ Anger creates negativity in your environment even when not directed at you.

❖ The underlying causes of anger must be recognized and acknowledged. When confronting an angry person, it's more effective to state how it bothers you.

❖ Accusations make an angry person angrier.

❖ Your husband may not realize the negative effect his anger has on you. Tell him, but he'll probably need to figure out the real cause of his anger on his own.

If your husband appears unable or unwilling to work with you to abet his anger, it may be time for you to insist on counseling—for both of you or for yourself.

> *"When an inner situation is not made conscious,*
> *it appears outside as fate."*
> **– Carl Young**

Coping Secrets from Other Wives

Helen complained that her husband's source of anger was the current political situation. He would rant and rave every time he heard a newscast. She knew his anger wasn't directed at her, but his rancor filled the air with negative energy. Fred thought it a bit strange when Helen asked him not to listen to newscasts while she was at home, but she explained that his negativity, even though not directed at her, made her feel tense and sick to her stomach. Because he didn't want to see her suffer, he tried to go for a walk while listening to the news on his cell phone. When Helen is at home he strives to redirect his energy into something more positive than ranting at newscasters.

Dennis didn't want to be difficult, but he didn't know why he felt so angry all the time. Joyce knew that it was making her feel miserable. Still she realized it wouldn't do much good to get angry back at him. It depressed her when he shot off some angry epitaph or accusation, but she refused to spend the rest of her life living in a sea of anger. While making a list of the effects of his rage and irritability on her, she was able to recognize some sources of his outbursts and decided to discuss them in a caring and calm conversation. She didn't plan to tell Dennis what was wrong or make him think she was trying to psychoanalyze him; she simply wanted him to see that he was hurting her.

Though taken back by her approach, Dennis recognized that she offered her comments to help him identify the why's and the when's of his malcontent. Once he started to recognize the sources of his outbursts, he was able to come out of denial and start solving the problem.

*"A positive attitude may not solve
all your problems, but it will annoy enough people
to make it worth the effort."*
– **Herm Albright, quoted in** *Reader's Digest*, **June 1995.**

Chapter Five

The Doesn't Ever Listen Husband

© Randy Glasbergen - glasbergen.com

"I'm trying to be a good listener, but you keep breaking my concentration by talking!"

Throughout the years men have developed the extraordinary skill of non-listening. Male researchers have documented this phenomena yet, with indomitable spirit, women keep striving to crack the syndrome.

Almost every woman I interviewed, regardless of her situation, noted lack of listening as a major marital issue. However, few called it a new retirement bone of contention...probably because it's something wives typically have dealt with throughout their marriage. Women tend to agree that most men are inherently unable to listen to a sustained conversation.

Women's intuition about this non-listening phenomena is backed up by studies confirming that women generally communicate more effectively than men. Studies show that men and women don't think alike because our brains are wired differently, especially when it comes to expressing emotions.[7] Imagine all the money scientists could have saved on research if they had just asked wives.

Nancy's Story: Why Can't I Share with Him?

"I thoroughly enjoyed the evening with my girlfriends and couldn't wait to tell Joe all about it," Nancy said. "When I got home he was—guess what—watching a ball game, so I waited. I figured he'd be eager to hear all about it. He even asked how my evening was when half-time came. So I launched into my description."

Nancy told him what everyone was wearing, then about Missy's new car. She was pleased when Joe smiled and seemed to listen, but it was only for a minute or so until she noticed his eyes wandering—checking out the screen and who knows what else. Just as she got to the really interesting part about the movie, he turned his head completely toward the screen, and that's when she stopped talking. When he turned to her about a minute later, and said, "So what else?", Nancy lost it.

"What else?" she said. "Have you heard anything? Did you even realize I was talking to you? Why do you never listen? Don't you know that part of the fun of an evening like I had with friends is sharing it with someone later? Can't you *ever* listen," she cried.

As you can imagine, things spiraled downward from there. However, even in her frustration, Nancy began to think seriously about how differently she and her husband approached a conversation, and she vowed to make some changes.

Ideas on how to reframe a discussion to meet both of your needs in the Survival Tips of this chapter helped Nancy and may help bring you closer to bliss in your retirement marriage.

Behind the Errant Behavior

The wiring difference in men's and women's brains plays a significant role in memory, hearing, vision and emotion—and in how we communicate.

Women tend to focus on how to create a solution that works for the group; they talk through issues, and utilize non-verbal cues such as tone, emotion, and empathy. This seems to make our communication more effective because everyone feels involved. Men, on the other hand, tend to be more task-oriented, less talkative, more isolated and want to give their own immediate idea for a solution, often leaving others to feel uninvolved in the process. Did you know studies show that men use only half their brain to listen?[8]

Aside from the biological differences in our brain wiring, there is a psychological difference that also affects our contrasting listening styles. Both men and women employ selective listening habits in their conversations and often block out unpleasant information, but women generally use up to 25 percent more words than men do. This use of what the male perceives as unnecessary words gives him an opportunity to filter out or ignore the words he finds unpleasant, demanding or threatening. That means when your husband employs that technique, he isn't hearing what you think is important.

Psychologist also say that men's tendency to tune out is often a function of their egos. Men tend to believe more strongly than women that they are always correct and will either avoid or ignore conversation that might prove differently. Since this ego tendency seems to be formed *in utero*, it can be a difficult one to purge, but probably worth some effort.

When it comes to the nitty gritty, however, most women feel that the real reason men don't listen is because they would just rather watch a ball game then talk about the problems of the world.

Your Spousal Right: To Be Listened To and Be HEARD

How often have you felt that your husband is just nodding or giving you the *uh huh* response and not hearing a word you're saying? If it's not a life threatening issue at that very moment, or if it is the last minute in a tie game, his non-listening might possibly be forgiven. However, if you do all the things counselors suggest—making sure you don't barrage him with words while he's in the middle of something important to him, picking your words with care, skipping a lot of what he may deem as superfluous words and, most of all, no nagging—it's not unreasonable for you to expect to have an adult conversation with him. Expectations and reality can differ, however, so it may take a bit of work before you reach your level of acceptance for what we women like to call adult conversation.

> *"We don't see things as they are,*
> *we see things as we are."*
> **– Anais Nin**

Survival Tips for All Wives

After reading this appalling information about the state of men's listening skills, you might feel there is no hope of ever being heard by your husband. But don't give up. If you want to talk about his listening skills (or lack thereof) think about how it makes you feel when he appears to wander off into space in the middle of your comments. Consider the best way to say what needs to be said, then say it. It's also helpful to consider how *he* might feel about *your* comments. This isn't to say you can predict his every thought, but if you reflect on how the conversation might go based on *his* response, it could help you manage the conversation in the direction *you* feel it should go. The following thoughts about the conversation styles of men and women will help: Men are task oriented and want to solve problems without superfluous conversation.

* To increase your husband's attention span, reduce the number of words you use.

* Be precise–global accusations such as "you never..." will lead him to reject everything you say...he DID take the garbage out three weeks ago.

* Word pictures are a great tool for male-female conversations.[9] Rather than, "I feel hurt," try "I feel as if I've been hit with a Mack Truck when you don't listen."

* Pick a time when it should be possible for him to give attention to the conversation–not while he's watching a ball game.

* You have the right to be heard.

* Stick with one issue and state it confidently and calmly.

* Many men may think women talk too much.

"He never listens to anything I say."
– Wife with a Husband Who Never Listens

Coping Secrets from Other Wives

When Janet began to feel particularly petulant about her husband not listening, she developed an awareness tactic. As his eyes started to glaze over or wander, she sensed that Harold hadn't heard her last ten or twelve words and stopped in the middle of the conversation. The first time she did that, his eyes came back to the room after a while and, looking a bit bewildered, asked if she was OK. She told him yes, but that from then on, she was going to stop talking every time she felt the conversation had ended because he wasn't listening. Over the next month–or three–Harold began to realize how often Janet sensed his less than stellar attention to her brilliant statements and now makes a noble effort to pay more attention.

"He went to the store to get the ingredients for salsa," Nancy said. "I asked him to get three tomatoes, one onion, a red pepper and the chips. He came home with one of each."

"Do you ever hear what I say?" Nancy asked.

"You never said *three* tomatoes," George replied.

"You didn't listen for *three*," Nancy said. "Besides...you've had this salsa before and you KNOW it's heavy on tomatoes."

As Nancy reminded George about the number of tomatoes in the salsa, she saw recognition in his eyes. It seemed to say he realized that he should have gotten three of them. He agreed to go back to the store for more because he really wanted the salsa. Nancy was happy that he realized he doesn't always listen as well as he might and that the number of tomatoes in the salsa didn't become an argument.

Note: Just for Fun: In my research on this topic I also came across a book that has a truly humorous take on the differences of men and woman. If you want a really good (albeit sardonic) laugh you might check out *Why Men Don't Listen and Women Can't Read Road Maps* by Barbara and Allan Pease.

"There's a big misconception that men do not want to hear. It is more accurate to say, they do not dare to feel."
– Anais *"Book Beat"* television show, iUniverseNin

PART II

NAVIGATING FROM SURVIVING TO THRIVING

We're looking for someone who can fly with the eagles, swim with the sharks and run with the wolves.

I can't fly, swim or run, but an eagle can't close a deal, a shark can't charm a client, and a wolf can't inspire a sales team!

Now that we have discussed (and suitably torn apart) the state of the male ego and his needs in retirement...and having empathized with one another on the challenges that often arise in a retirement marriage, let's explore some lifelines that will help you move from just surviving to thriving in your relationship.

In the last chapter we saw that there are no more important life preservers for marriage then listening well and sharing your deepest thoughts. Let those tips guide you as you and your husband share your dreams for retirement.

> *"My mission in life is not merely to survive,*
> *but to thrive; and to do so with some passion,*
> *some compassion, some humor, and some style."*
> **– Maya Angelou**

Chapter Six

Focus On The Positive

"The FDA has classified compliments as an essential nutrient."

A significant contribution to success as a couple comes from sharing your personal dreams, hopes and goals with one another. The act of sharing dreams requires a great deal of attentive listening and often leads to enjoyable conversations. Over the years, however, these skills may have been put aside while you were busy raising a family, getting to work and maintaining a home. Still, you no doubt shared your dreams in some form during your courtship and early marriage for we are usually drawn to someone who has similar goals and outlooks on life.

Dreams spark our imaginations and incite us to action, but without them life is like a boat without a rudder. They are our buoys that keep us from moving aimlessly, blown about by the wind, driven by the currents, and off course most of the time.

An important ingredient in the sharing of dreams with your spouse is the sense of comfort and trust you have in your relationship. Freely giving deserved compliments brings you closer. It shows your spouse that you value what he or she says and does. Best of all, receiving and giving praise nourishes our hearts and makes us smile.

It doesn't cost anything to dream or to give compliments, but taking the time to focus on them adds zest to our lives.

*"If you're thinking it might be difficult
to wish your husband peace, especially when you're feeling
annoyed with him, you're probably right. That's why it
[reflective thinking or meditation] is called a practice."*
– Alan Lokos

Dorothy's Story: Where There's a Problem, There's a Solution

Doug had seemed reasonably content in his new retirement life. After the first year, however, cleaning out the garage, the basement and the attic *and* creating the perfect lawn in their small yard lost its excitement. He started moping around and Dorothy worried that he seemed to have lost his energy and enthusiasm for life.

Prior to his retirement Doug and Dorothy had occasionally dreamt about how they would spend their retirement days, but now Doug wasn't sure where to begin. He told Dorothy that he couldn't figure out what he would enjoy or what they could possibly afford. Dorothy reminded Doug that he used to dream of sailing around the world, but he responded that they had no boat. He also mumbled that, since he hadn't sailed since he was a teenager, that dream was impossible

"Perhaps you won't get to sail around the world next week," Dorothy said, "but a small sail boat isn't that expensive–and wouldn't you want to start with a small one to remember how to sail first?" "Besides," she kidded him, "think of the money you'll save on fertilizer and grass seed when you're too occupied to fret over a brown spot in the lawn."

Doug was intrigued by her idea, so he decided to go boat shopping. That, in itself, was a good experience; he and Dorothy spent several *Date Days* visiting various harbors while searching for a used sail boat. Eventually they found one that met their needs exactly. It was in pretty good shape with room enough for the two of them and for friends or grandchildren to join them occasionally–but small enough for him to mange on his own.

Once they brought the boat home, Doug seemed to come alive again. He decided to take a sailing safety course to renew his knowledge of the sport and remember the basics about owning a boat. When he wasn't studying and relearning the rigging terms, he was preparing the boat for their first spring outing. That summer Dorothy and Doug explored all the lakes and rivers near their home and acknowledged that it was almost as good as going around the world since they had never been to these spots on the water before.

"You can be as happy as you make up your mind to be."
– Wife with an Attitude for Success

Carol's Story: The Joy of Compliments

The first year of retirement marriage was pretty miserable for Carol and Dennis. "I couldn't figure out what was happening," Carol told me one day over coffee. "We just seemed to annoy one another and constantly got in each other's way. Even the sound of him shuffling his slippers through the house drove me nuts," she continued. "You would have thought he could have picked up his feet–he's not that old," she mused aloud.

When I asked Carol what happened to make them seem so compatible now, she launched into the most remarkable–but amazingly simple–story of what turned their marriage around.

Her smile revealed her happiness as she said, "We started complimenting one another."

Carol told me the compliment fest hadn't happened overnight, but she was amazed at the change in their relationship after she or Dennis, she wasn't sure who, insisted that they had to talk about what they were doing to one another and do something about how miserable they felt together.

Carol felt that the key to their turn around was realizing the harm they were doing to one another. Neither one of them was the sole culprit, and they had to solve this problem together.

"We talked about what annoyed each of us and how it might change," Carol said. "Often what changed was just understanding each other's reason for doing something in a particular way or at a particular time."

Once Carol or Dennis understood the reason behind a certain action, their perception of the problem also usually changed. She delighted in telling me how their awareness made compromise so much easier.

As we continued talking, Carol told me how she had cultivated an attitude of gratitude and finding something to be grateful for every day had a remarkable effect on their relationship. After she and Dennis agreed to stop hurting one another with complaints and unkind statements, she started realizing that she had much to be grateful for. Carol decided to be conscious of two things she was grateful for every day. Doing this made her see that many of the good things in her life were connected to her relationship with Dennis, and she began to compliment him regularly.

"*And,* since kindness is contagious," she said, "he started noticing reasons to compliment me. Best of all, since we both feel good about ourselves and one another it's so much easier to want to do things together. Now it's exciting to dream and create new ideas or projects that will keep us active, healthy, and happy in our retirement years. Much better than living in a sea of misery," Carol declared.

Creating Positive Results

If you're still breathing you probably still have dreams. If they're missing from your life, it could it be that you are swimming in a sea of hopelessness with all the negativity around home—or have you given up your ability to make decisions? Has your husband done that as well? Now may be the perfect time for you and your life-mate to rediscover your ability to dream and renew your sharing.

Just as it did for Carol and Dennis, taking the time to compliment one another could bring zest into your relationship and make you more comfortable sharing with one another again. Who doesn't feel good after receiving even the smallest of compliments?[10] If only for a moment, it turns our attention away from anything sour in our lives and slips a bit of joy into our existence.

Right now, if your husband is going through an angry or bossy stage, it might be difficult to even think about giving him a compliment let alone coming up with a deserved one. However, thinking of it as an investment in your future, as well as for his, will help you find at least one thing a day that is worth a positive comment.

Compliments provided on a regular basis, could prompt him to put aside his anger and move him to do something about his negative attitude.

Admittedly, if you feel your husband is totally set in ways that make you miserable, you might wonder why you should encourage him to dream, but I hope you'll consider this possibility. You can't set his goals, but you might at least encourage him to take a look at why he has lost sight of creating something meaningful or joyful for himself.

Couple's Right: To Dream, Create New Goals and Give Compliments

In the movie, *South Pacific*, Bloody Mary tells us we need dreams for they make us happy and give meaning to our lives. That thought has inspired me since I was a teenager because I realized that dreams feed our goals. As young people we dreamt about when we would graduate from high school or when we would turn twenty-one—or maybe when we would marry or finish graduate school.

Whatever dreams we held, they fed our ambition to do things, to succeed at something and probably to learn something. They gave meaning to our lives. Even though we may have a few wrinkles on our faces now, we're really no different than the young person we were years ago. We still need dreams. Without them we relinquish our sense of personal power and our ability to make decisions for ourselves. If you and your husband can renew (or start) the practice of discussing and creating mutual dreams, you're likely to find a depth in your relationship that can lead you to a new understanding of one another and an avenue to joy in retirement.

Giving and receiving compliments is also an avenue for creating mutual happiness and something you both have the right to expect. Graciously receiving a compliment is important, for we sometimes forget that when a person gives you a compliment he or she is giving you part of themselves. If we negate their observation, we also negate their worth, so gratefully receiving a compliment makes both the giver and the receiver feel good. When you give or graciously receive a compliment, you're sharing your delight in your husband's efforts to accomplish something of value to you

The following thoughts will help you move from surviving to thriving as a caring couple:

❋ Kindness is contagious.

❋ Give and receive compliments; it's good for your heart.

❋ Find daily reasons to say thank you or give a compliment.

❋ Dreaming together makes it easier to negotiate how you will spend your retirement.

❋ The more couples share their dreams, the richer their lives become.

❋ Dreams help us reach attainable goals.

❋ It's never too late to dream.

Success Secrets from a Happy Wife

Sharon and Gary retired together. He had been a Health and Science teacher in middle school, and she had been a high school counselor. They planned to spend their retirement days pursuing the many interests they had discussed over the years. There was only one problem. While they both had travel plans, Gary wanted to go on an adventure every month, but Sharon was also looking for downtime to write about their travels and the book she had been planning for years. Gary's idea of traveling also included extreme adventures such as skiing a glacier in Valdez, Alaska, and Sharon thought about something tamer such as cruising the Amazon River.

Their compromise...Sharon brought her computer when the traveled and, while Gary enjoyed activities that had no appeal to her, she found a comfortable space where she could write. This allowed her to express her creativity, but they were still able to travel together as they had always planned.

CHAPTER SEVEN

REKINDLE THE LOVE

What's the point of arguing if nobody keeps
score and the winner doesn't get a trophy?!"

Sometimes you and your husband might find that when he gives up a life-time of work and schedules, life isn't as wonderful as either of you thought it would be.

You may start to feel the pain of his stress if your retired husband expresses a sense of detachment, loneliness, anger or hopelessness. But this is not the time for either of you to give up on life; nor is it the time for him to become totally dependent on you. It may be time, however, to consider how you relate to one another.

Focusing on a mutual desire to achieve happiness can help you work toward that blissful retirement marriage I think we all sought—and probably expected—when we first said, "I do."

In Part I of this book we focused on the necessity of caring for yourself and being clear about your needs, but truthfully, the full secret to a successful retirement marriage is mutual caring and respect for one another. This is especially true when you are negotiating difficult issues.

The first step toward mutual respect is becoming skillful listeners. This is usually best accomplished when you remind yourselves that you do care for your spouse, despite the current turmoil (You must...you've spent all those years together) and that it's to your mutual benefit to respect one another.

Vivian's Story: The Power of Caring

Vivian smiled when I told her the title of this book. "I've got to read it," she said. "You know, when my husband David first retired, I couldn't get over the fact that he was *always there*–always interrupting my routine." She told me (as so many wives have already said) that she felt angry when he infringed on her space. It also annoyed her that he seemed to expect her to be there to do what he needed, when he needed it. *And,* most especially, it irritated her when he'd call from another room and ask where such and such was–even when it was right in front of him.

After a while though, Vivian asked herself why she was being so territorial and began to realize that it was his space too. "True," she said, "I was the one who had decorated the house and created a comfortable place for us to live, but he contributed his share to the process. Besides our home had been intended for both of us so I had to relearn how to share. It wasn't easy because it had been *my space* for years–David went off to work, and I took care of the home."

Then Vivian focused on solutions that worked for them. She told me they discovered that each of them would be happier if they had some space to themselves, so they staked out their own areas of escape, and the rest of the house was shared. David loves his workshop and Vivian enjoys her quiet space for quilting and reading.

"That works pretty well," Vivian said. "Now that I have my escape hatch, however, we find ourselves wanting to be in the common area more often. I guess it's really more a matter of understanding one another's needs than it is about territory or routine."

"I'm glad we figured this out," Vivian continued. "My husband is not well now, and I want to make sure that all of our time together is happy and free from stress as much as possible."

I couldn't help but be amazed at how much Vivian taught me in just that five minute discussion. To me, her story defines the importance of listening well and the benefit of compromise. Most of all, I think it shows the value of caring for one another.

To care for one another is to love one another. "
– **A Wise Wife**

The following tips will help you move from surviving to thriving:

Success Tips for Caring Couples

❋ If you are always winning, the chances are, you are losing.[11]

❋ Take the time to listen to what your spouse is *really* saying.

❋ Do unto your spouse as you would have your spouse do unto you.

❋ Kindness, compassion, unselfish joy and serenity are ideal tools for caring.

❋ A positive caring relationship makes it easier to deal with adversity.

❋ Wish the other person good thoughts when disagreements arise.

Success Secret from a Persistent Wife

Barbara wanted to scream every time Roy interrupted her mid–sentence. She was starting to feel incompetent as he developed the habit of telling her she was wrong even before she finished her thought. In time, she began to wonder if he valued anything she said or did.

Instead of getting angry at what she perceived to be his rudeness, Barbara learned to take a deep breath, smile pleasantly and say, "Thank you dear, I don't know how I managed to say anything correctly before you retired."

The first few times this happened, Roy looked surprised, but murmured, "You're welcome." Now, after recognizing the pain in her comment, Roy agreed to keep his unsolicited corrections to himself because he didn't want to hurt her. Barbara has also helped Roy see that, when he simply can't contain himself from giving advice, he *could* change the feeling and tone of the exchange by first asking if he *might* make a suggestion.

Chapter Eight

Make Your Retirement Marriage Work

"I was in a good mood once, but I couldn't find any practical use for it."

A s you read through sections of this book you may have occasionally wondered, "Why do I need to do all the work? He's the one who's being bossy, dependent, selfish and angry." That's a natural feeling for it probably feels that it's your husband who's causing the problems–he's the one who came home after all.

Regardless of the careers we have chosen for our life work, it seems that, as women, we are hard-wired to care for others. It's a pretty safe bet that at some point in life you assumed the role of teacher or care-giver–so why not do that now when you can be the major beneficiary of your efforts? Bringing laughter, love and compassion to your marriage will be contagious. Even a grumpy old man can't ignore this infectious disease in your home. It's the best prescription for a blissful retirement marriage, regardless of your finances, your health or where you live.

Researchers have found that happily married older couples highly value their relationships and experience increasing closeness as the years go by. Nonetheless, when retirement time arrives, there are many things that need to be worked out. Enjoying one another in retirement doesn't happen overnight; the necessary adjustments require great effort and practice. While each person needs time for privacy and personal interests, creating time together is important as well. Irritations need to be resolved, and having open communication, flexibility and humor can help minimize conflict. Finally, retirement can be a time for great personal development and for creating enjoyable, rewarding relationships with old and new friends.

After reading all forms of books, blogs, newsletters, and newspapers and talking with numerous wives with retired husbands, I discovered there are just a few basic principles to bring bliss to retirement marriages. If you or your husband are soon retiring, you've probably been married long enough to have heard much of this advice before. Sometimes, however, solutions hide from us when we're in the throes of conflict or adjustment so I offer a few for your consideration. What would you add as tips for moving from surviving to thriving as a couple?

Success Tips for Caring Couples

✳ In most cases it takes two to tango.

✳ It's futile to blame your partner for your lack of happiness or self-worth. No one is perfect, but love and empathy support a marriage.

✳ You earned the right for bliss, but you have to create it.

✳ There are two sides to every story.

✳ You look younger when you smile.

✳ Retirement has the potential to be the best stage of married life.

Success Secret from This Wife of a Retired Husband

A Personal Story: Like many couples, my husband and I struggled when he first retired. It wasn't so much his more frequent presence in our home as it was my perception of the change in my schedule that his presence entailed. Before retiring, Art traveled frequently for work or left for the office at an early hour. Now, like most, he wanted to sleep a bit later. However, morning was still my favorite time of the day, and I was eager to get up before the rest of the world. This created a problem for me because I felt guilty when I woke him leaving the room.

The kitchen area presented another complication. The counter top, designed to serve as his desktop for the few days he worked from home, now held his computer and paper work all the time. That might have been OK except when not used as a desk, it also served as my spillover cooking space. Instead of asking him to move his stuff on the rare occasions I cooked up a storm, I fumed and worried about spilling something on the computer.

Art also had his issues. Just as he finally got excited about having time to pursue other interests, he was asked to stay on part time to close out the US plant and oversee the foreign operations. He fully understood the difficulties he would face, while the rest of us did not. Consequently, he wasn't eager to take on this responsibility. Despite the many reasons he didn't want to assume this position, he reluctantly succumbed to the encouragement of many people—including me. Resolving the problems he had anticipated took more time and energy than he had agreed to. This led him to feel angry about the situation, and at me for having encouraged him to take it on.

I could list other complaints from both of us, but you get the picture. Fortunately, after a fair amount of stress, we realized that we'd been in this gig they call marriage for a very long time and ought to take steps to make it work again. We started talking and clarified our perceptions and retirement issues. We agreed that, although we'd like to think growing old was a long time away for us, it would be better to do it together and lovingly. Today, that thought makes it easier for us to find the good in one another and share our delight in being together, even day in and day out.

We practiced all of the things I've written about such as, not criticizing, balancing time together and apart, finding activities we enjoy independently and together, dealing with anger, listening to one another, and most importantly, caring for one another.

My prayer...May you find the same delight in being together.

"The key to retirement is to find joy in the little things."
- Susan Miller

PART III

CREATE NEW VISIONS

glasbergen.com

GLASBERGEN

"Do you really think 3D glasses can
bring greater depth to our relationship?"

In Parts I and II we discussed common difficulties couples face
when first retired and strategies they used to resolve them. Part
III describes long-held dreams of a few individuals I had the good
fortune to come to know through my research. Their stories reveal
concerns they had while planning for their dreams. These ideas may
not match your particular needs; for instance, skiing five mountains
on five continents in five years may hold no interest for you, but the
compromises Ted and his wife needed to make deserve your consideration.

Retirement marriage brings opportunities not typically available to couples in their first stage of newly married bliss or in the
second stage when building careers and families. This third stage
offers the freedom and responsibility to choose for yourself how
you want to spend your time and resources, while growing in your
joy of *being together*.

The following stories are intended to inspire you and your spouse to dream and have great conversations about plans for your mutual retirement journey.

CHAPTER NINE

IMAGINE YOUR JOURNEY

"Spend less time earning a living,"
and more time earning a loving."

John's Story: A Lifeline for Others

John spent most of his career working with teenagers who had severe behavior challenges. He saw a good deal of destructive behavior but never gave up believing in the potential of these young men to live law-abiding and fulfilling lives. He knew what they needed and helped many of them turn their lives around.

John was torn by the thought of leaving these young men when he retired, so he and his wife Jean explored how he could stay connected with the youth and still enjoy their time together. Jean understood his dilemma but hoped he wouldn't decide to return to work. As they discussed her concern, they discovered a plan for him to help these young men while still having time for them to share their many mutual interests.

John began writing for their local newspaper about the struggles many youth faced. He showed readers how young people can be thrown to the courts for simple misdemeanors or be falsely accused because of their attire or circumstances. His readers came to see how the stigma of a police record or the interruption of an education makes it difficult for young people in these situations to create a productive adult life.

After John published several articles, a local resident contacted him hoping to help reduce the likelihood of local young men getting into trouble. The two men spent many months creating a plan for an effective mentoring program and managed to have it incorporated it into the town's youth program. John now spends two days a week at the center helping young men become productive members of society.

Becky's Story: Flying High

Becky always wanted to learn to fly. Her grandfather was a pilot. She flew across country with him as a young girl and never forgot the thrill of seeing America from a *bird's-eye perspective*.

In earlier stages of married life, Becky had a busy schedule. The challenges of raising three children along with her military husband's relocations made learning to fly an impossible dream. Still, whenever she saw a plane piercing through the clouds on a clear day, she vowed that someday she would fly a plane.

Becky and her husband Jim don't have a lot of money, but her energy and desire pushed her to find a way to make her dream of flying come true. Their friend Dave who owned the local airport was struggling to make ends meet. He depended on the landing fees of private planes, but the skyrocketing price of aviation fuel prompted many pilots to ground their aircraft.

Cost cutting measures forced Dave to let his bookkeeper go. Although sorry for his difficulties, Becky, an experienced bookkeeper, saw a way to make her dream come true while helping him. She approached Dave and suggested bartering her skills for flight instruction. Dave was delighted as her offer would give him more time to instruct students instead of struggling with the stress of keeping financial records. His only requirement was that Becky pay for the fuel used in her training flights.

Becky saw this as a small price to make her lifelong dream become reality. She began organizing Dave's accounts that very day, and he provided her with information she needed to study before her flight instruction began.

Becky, now retired, is on her way to receiving her pilot's license. Delighted for her opportunity to "pierce clouds from her pilot's seat," she and her husband Jim are busy planning trips to distant places together.

"What we think, we become.
All that we are arises with our thoughts.
With our thoughts, we make the world. "
- **Buddha**

Ted's Story: The Power of Good Planning

Ted, a systematic and highly energetic engineer, was eager to retire. He loved his work, but he craved variety and wished to pursue more activities than time allowed. At age 55, he began to make a list of all the ways he would spend his retirement. By age 65, his abundant list included target dates for accomplishing specific dreams.

An ardent skier and traveler, Ted decided that he wanted to ski five mountains on five continents in five years. His plan included the name of each mountain he would ski, the date he would ski each one and where he would stay on each journey. He was so organized that he made reservations for his first year a month before he retired.

Ted's wife Sharon supported his plan because, long before retirement, they had discussed what each of them wanted and the compromises they would make to accommodate one another. Ted and Sharon had moved numerous times in their early years together for Ted's work. Now Sharon is happy to have moved back to the area where their grown children and her siblings live

In Ted's absence Sharon fills her day painting and enjoying her sisters, children and grandchildren. When asked about Ted's frequent travels she responds, "It may sound as if it's a lot of travel, but, it's really only a few weeks out of a whole year. "Besides," she said, "it's good for our marriage for each of us to have our own interests.

*"Retirement has been a discovery of beauty for me.
I never had the time before to notice
the beauty of my grandkids, my wife,
the tree outside my very own front door,
and, the beauty of time itself.*
– Author unknown

Planning Tips for Your Retirement

❉ It's important to remember that the only right plan
is the one that meets the needs of both you and your
mate.

❉ Give yourself time to think about your true desires.

❉ Forget SOMEDAY. Imagine what could be possible
TODAY

❉ Give yourself permission to change your mind and your
plans.

❉ Compromise to lay the groundwork for harmony

❉ Rediscover one another

Part IV

Chart Your Journey

©Randy Glasbergen
glasbergen.com

"I'm trying fo find a hacker who can get inside my
husband's brain and tell me what's on his mind."

While researching for this book, I heard concerns from many people about retiring. Some questioned how they would spend their time. Others feared they would miss the friends they had made at work, or that they would not have enough money to do what they would like to do in retirement.

The concern I heard most consistently, however, was sheer horror at spending so much time with one's spouse. Many of us feel guilty having these feelings and are ashamed to admit it. However, if your concern about sharing more time together or you fear that your spouse will interfere with your routine isn't discussed, it will be difficult to embrace this new stage in your marriage and enjoy one another's company

Part I of this book, contained stories of couples who struggled with togetherness early in retirement and how they found solutions for their situations. Do you remember Vivian's Story, *The Power of Caring* in Part II? Vivian felt anger when her husband David first retired because he often infringed on her space. They finally talked about the issue and created private places in their home for each of them plus a room to enjoy together. She found it interesting that, once they had their personal areas, both of them gravitated more often to the common space. "Perhaps the solitude helped them appreciate one another's company," she said.

Vivian was especially happy they had accomplished this because David now has serious health concerns, and she wants to treasure every moment with him.

Studies have shown that, as we grow older, we grow in appreciation of our mates. Clearly this is what happened to Vivian and David, and it can happen for you as well.

Still other soon-to-be-retirees dread the loss of contact with colleagues, or are fearful of how they will spend their retirement days. If that's your concern, it will be important to plan how you will stay connected with those friends. In may be as simple as getting together regularly for dinner, a sporting or theatre event or even meeting at the gym. Whatever it is, that plan will provide something to anticipate and enjoy. Now, with time to pursue your dreams, you are also likely to cultivate new friendships with individuals who have similar retirement interests.

Still another common concern of couples approaching retirement is a fear of not having enough money to live as they would like. Since this is not a financial advice book, I won't go down that road, but I do encourage you to seek the guidance of a financial expert since our economic situation does impact our choices. It may also help to know that many of the couples who navigated successfully through their retirement adjustment shared the observation that good life planning helped them scale their dreams to match their finances. With a clear understanding of what was most important to them as a couple and as individuals, they were able to select affordable and achievable goals. Dorothy's story in Chapter Six, *Where There's A problem, There's A Solution*, may provide ideas for you.

Dorothy's husband Doug had dreamed of sailing around the world, but he had neither the experience nor the money to "captain" such a venture. Dorothy suggested that Doug might want to get a small boat and refresh his sailing skills as he hadn't sailed since his teens. After finding a used sailboat, Doug found satisfaction in refurbishing it and relearning knot tying and rigging skills. Now Doug and Dorothy spend many happy days sailing around local areas they would never have seen if they hadn't pursued Doug's dream. Perhaps the best way to fulfill your retirement dreams is to act on them. William Shakespeare once wrote, *"We are such stuff as dreams are made on."* That means YOU! You can be the *stuff* that your dreams are made on. Your retirement wish list may not be as detailed as Ted's, or as long held as Becky's but the map you and your spouse create will guide you into a harmonious retirement marriage.

> *"Married couples who enjoy spending time together and can confide in each other usually maintain a close and giving relationship as they age."*
> **– Suzanna Smith, StrongerMarriage.org**[12]

> *"Life is good now that we understand one another's needs*
> .- **Contented Wife with a Retired Husband**

CHAPTER TEN

SECURE YOUR RETIREMENT DREAMS

"After all these years, I still tingle
when you touch me. I'm not sure if it's
love or poor circulation."

There are many ways to identify and carry out your dreams for retirement. Consider an online class or workshop at your community's Adult Learning Program to help you and your spouse create a plan. Perhaps a workshop is too public a forum, but in-depth discussions with a close friend or family member may be another way for you to explore your hopes and dreams. Other couples prefer to let their imaginations run, listing activities they would like to pursue in retirement and identifying how they will overcome potential obstacles. Others have found success by just "winging it," as one quite happily retired friend told me.

"I'm not here because I'm supposed to be here,
or because I'm trapped here, but because
I'd rather be with you than anywhere in the world."
-Richard David Bach, Author

SUCCESSFUL RETIREMENT STEPS

As you and your spouse plan for your perfect retirement, you might find the following ideas helpful. The blank pages at the end of this book serve as a convenient place for you to write your thoughts and refer back to whenever you choose.

Step 1. Evaluate

An important step for you and your partner is to reflect on how each of you views your potential retirement situation. Do you expect retirement to change your life style? If so, how? What are your concerns about potential changes? What are your partner's concerns? How will you blend your concerns and dreams with one another?

Be honest with yourself and one another. If you ignore this step, you could encounter surprises along the way. Most people plan with specific expectations in mind, but if you are not aware that your expectations are different from your spouse's, it could become a bumpy journey for both of you.

Step 2. Assess Your Passions

Once you identify your expectations for retirement, consider your passions and how they fit into your retirement dreams. What did you hope to do with your life when you were 15, 25 or 45? Have you done any or all of these? Do you think any of your earlier dreams would still bring you joy and fulfillment? On a scale of 1-10, how much energy are you willing to put into accomplishing your dreams? How much time, money or support will you need? Remember, even if you don't have ALL the resources you think you might need, you could probably scale your desire to fit your means.

Step 3. Consider Your Creative Talents

Generally the things we enjoy doing most are those that make use of our given strengths. For example, I could never be a computer programmer because that requires linear thinking skills I simply do not possess. It would be torture (and a distinct failure) for me to sit in front of a computer in the effort to create an internet tool or some application for a smart phone. On the other hand, I could sit in front of a computer all day and write because, as a right-brained individual, this gives me pleasure. I developed my writing skills at various jobs earlier in my life, and now I am comfortable with my ability to string together readable sentences.

What do you consider your greatest talents and how would you bring them to life? After you and your mate have imagined all the hurdles that might get in your way, ask yourself if you want this badly enough to overcome those obstacles. If the answer is, "Yes," you likely will discover that there are fewer hurdles than you thought.

Step 4. Share Your Dreams
Again the importance of communication becomes apparent. If your spouse has no idea how you would like to spend your retirement years, one or both of you could be in for a big surprise, and that could lead to disharmony in the relationship. Sharing your dreams with your life mate also provides a tremendous opportunity for each of you to get to know one another better—even after all these years.

Before, or as you are considering, retiring, take some "dream dates." They're a perfect excuse to break out from the ordinary and go someplace new to share your thoughts about how retirement could transform your lives. As you share, be open to one another's ideas. There will be time later to consider the realities of implementing those dreams, but discussing your wildest and happiest thoughts could reveal ideas for a mutually gratifying future.

Step 5. Compare
Consider the similarities and differences in your wishes. How will your individual ambitions fit with your mutual hopes for a contented retirement marriage? What will each of you have to do to help your mate achieve his or her goals, and are you willing to take that action?

Step 6. Compromise
This step assures harmony in the relationship. If you want to start a new career and your mate hopes to sail around the world with you, how do you balance those desires? No matter how hard your spouse may try to adapt to your wishes, if he or she is deeply disappointed over your retirement choices, it will be more difficult to achieve a mutually happy retirement.

Step 7. Take Action – No Matter How Small It Is.

Now, that you have shaken the dust off old dreams–or created new ones– imagine how you will feel when you take action toward accomplishing them. Will you feel excited? Will you feel 20 years younger? Will you have a sense of fulfillment and delight in what you will achieve? You won't find out until you do it!

> **Note:** For a thorough and interactive approach to creating your dream retirement, visit:
> www.surviveyourhusbandsretirement.com
>
> Consider taking a workshop or using one of our worksheets which are available on request by emailing:
> nora@surviveyourhusband'sretirement.com

"Desire is the key to motivation,
but it's determination and commitment
to an unrelenting pursuit of your goal -
a commitment to excellence - that will enable you
to attain the success you seek.
– Mario Andretti

CHAPTER ELEVEN

ARRIVE AT YOUR PORT OF CALL

"The secret to a long marriage?
Never get divorced!"

In order for you and your spouse to pursue your collective dreams, both of you will have to give serious consideration to where you will live in retirement. The home you chose when you were younger is likely filled with happy memories, but it may not be the right space once retired. Is it too big, too expensive or too remote, too quiet, too noisy, or does it have too many stairs? Would you simply like to live someplace else?

Your place of residence may impact your plans. Regulations of a condo association can hinder hopes of creating a two-acre garden. Time and financial constraints could hinder your goal to spend time with family if you must travel to the other side of the country to visit. After defining your retirement goals, consider how your home's location will enhance or obstruct your plans.

For many, climate is an important consideration. Have you "had it" with snow and winter or do you want to spend this season with easy access to winter sports? Do you want to live in a city, the country, the suburbs, in a free-standing home, an apartment or a condo? How much can you afford for housing, and how much space do you want? How much proximity do you want to your friends and family?

The time and effort spent considering these questions will guide you to your perfect destination. The stories below might help you consider your priorities for where you will live.

James' and Martha's Story: It's a Question of Priorities[13]

Martha and James knew where they lived in retirement would affect their contentment and ability to do things that mattered to them so they began asking serious questions of one another. How much could they afford for housing? How much would they pay in taxes if they stayed where they are and what they would pay if they moved? How often did they want to be with their children? What kind of home did they want if they moved? Was weather important? How did they want to spend their time? They also discussed what they loved about their present home and what they would like to change. This process enabled them to identify most of their priorities, and they began to calmly discuss relocation or staying put.

After many conversations they realized that although they loved living on the north east coast of Maine, it was time to find a place that allowed more opportunity for gardening, biking, boating, walks on the beach and outdoor grilling. They wanted to be in a place where spring lasted longer than two weeks. They also sought to be in an area with access to theatre and opportunities for community service. San Diego became their ideal consideration, but they realized it would be too far and too expensive to regularly visit their children on the East coast. With their priorities identified, they explored other areas and picked the eastern shore of Maryland as their first choice.

Next they had to decide what type of home they wanted and could afford. They haven't settled on a residence yet, but they have made several trips to the area, renting for a week or two at a time. After narrowing their choices to two towns and identifying their desired neighborhoods and type of home, they are working with a real estate broker who notifies them when something of interest to them comes on the market.

"And suddenly you know: It's time
to start something new and trust the magic of beginnings."
– Meister Eckhart, German philosopher, theologian

Michael and Judith's Story: Staying Where We Landed

Michael and Judith moved into their home 48 years ago, two months before their first son was born. At the time it had all the space they needed, and when their next two sons came into the family, they added a second floor with two more bedrooms and a bath. Over the years, Michael completed several renovations that made their home even more comfortable. Judith is fond of the windows he added in the kitchen eating area because they invite the sun in each morning and enrich the plants sitting on the windowsill. Their yard is also a source of joy with vegetable and flower gardens throughout.

As much as they loved their home, Michael and Judith still considered moving. However, after focusing on their proximity to life-long friends, family, their church and a beautiful city twenty minutes away, they asked one another why they would even consider a move.

The house had the exact amount of space they needed. By adding a door and a separate heating system for the upstairs bedrooms they minimized their heating requirements while staying warm and comfortable downstairs. That made the house just big enough for the two of them and, on the flip side, when grandchildren come to visit, all they have to do is open the door and turn on the heat.

When passion and skill work together,
the end result is often a masterpiece
– Chris Guillebeau, The $100 Startup

Note: Chris Guillebeau's quote seems to sum up the reality of creating a joyful and contented retirement marriage. What you and your mate do to create your perfect retirement will be different from that of anyone else, and it might not always be easy. However, your mutual desire to create happiness can lead you to rediscovering one another and create a happy retirement marriage that works for both of you.

Cherish the fact that you have a teammate in life, because the difference it makes is impossible to overestimate.
– Andrea Syrtash, Author

THE SEVEN COMMANDMENTS OF RETIREMENT MARRIAGE

Thou Shall Not Give Copious Commands

Thou Shall Not Hover

Thou Shall Explore New Activities

Thou Shall Temper Your Temper

Thou Shall Listen

Thou Shall Share Dreams and Compliments

Thou Shall Care for One Another

৵৹

Suggested Reading

Coontz, Stephanie. *Marriage, A History; from Obedience to Intimacy or How Love Conquered Marriage.* Penguin Group, 2005.

Bernard, Dave. *I Want To Retire! Essential Considerations for the Retiree to Be.* CreateSpace Independent Publishing Platform, 2013

Bombeck, Erma. *A Marriage Made in Heaven or Too Tired For An Affair.* Harper Torch, 1994.

Gelb, Alan. Having *The Last Say: Capturing Your Legacy in One Small Story.* Jeremy P. Tarcher/Penguin, 2015.

Laura, Robert. *Naked Retirement.* Spiritus Publishing, 2009.

Pease, Barbara and Allan. *Why Men Don't Listen and Women Can't Read Maps.* Broadway Books, 1998.

Simsion, Gaeme. *The Rosie Project.* Simon & Schuster, 2013.

Strobel, Monica. *The Compliment Quotient.* Wise Rose Press, 2011.

WORKS CITED

1. Tournier, Paul. http://foryourmarriage.org/everymarriage/stages-of-marriage. [retrieved, March 16, 2011]

2. Myers and Booth 1996. *"Retirement Influences on Marital and Family Relations."* http://family.jrank.org/pages/1406/Retirement-Retirement-Influences-on-Marital-Family. [retrieved March 16, 2011]

3. Grey, John. *Men Are from Mars, Women are From Venus.* Harper Collins, 1992. p. 48

4. Bochner, Daniel A, Ph.D. *Women and Men.* http://drbochner.com/articles_for_couples/women_and_men. [retrieved 5/14/13]

5. Carnes, David. *"Positive Attitude Vs. Negative Attitude."* http://www.livestrong.com/article/140560-positive-attitude-vs-negative attitude/#. [retrieved 11/20/12]

6. *Medical News Today.* http://www.medicalnewstoday.com/releases/24551.php. [retrieved 11/15/12]

7. *Women's Health Magazine.* *"Understanding Men."* http://www.womenshealthmag.com/sex-and-relationships/understanding-men [retrieved 7/31/2012]

8. Hotz, Robert Lee. Los Angeles Times, *"Women Use More of Brain When Listening."* 11/29/2000. http:// articles.latimes.com/2000/nov/29/news/mn-58786. [retrieved 8/17/16].

9. Elliott, Belinda. CBN.com. *"Get Your Husband to Listen to You."* http://www1.cbn.com/marriage/getyour-husband-to-listen-to-you. [retrieved 8/17/16]

10. Lokos, Allan. Patience, *The Art of Peaceful Living.* Penguin Books, 2012.

11. Ibid.

12. Smith, Suzanne. *Family Relationships in Later Life.* http://www.strongermarriage.org/married/familyrelationships-in-later-life. [retrieved 8/25/16].

13. Edleson, Harriet. *New York Times.* "*For Older Couples, House Hunting Begins With Soul Searching.*" http://www.nytimes.com/2014/08/16/your-money/for-older-couples-house-hunting-beginswith-soul-searching.html? [retrieved 8/17/16.

Acknowledgments

Kudos to my husband, Art, for his unending support and for the impetus to create this book.

Thanks to Lisa Tener, Founder of Bring Your Book To Life, for her friendship and for coaching me on how to write a good story; to Arielle Eckstut of The Book Doctors for her sage advice and for convincing me of the absolute need for this book and to Amy Rose for her incredible editing skills. And what would a book be without the help and patience of good friends such as Carol Thomas and Mary Sue Bunting who plowed through the first edition and generously offered constructive suggestions and Lee Karwoski who proofed the final copy and gave it her Imprimatur.

I am indebted to Martha Langer of Pear Ink Design, Martha Rhodes who inspired this second edition and to Michael Grossman of EBook Bakery. Their commitment to working together to create the new look and feel of this book has been the perfect example of creative genius.

Finally, where would this book be without the generous sharing of so many women with retired husbands? To all of you, thank you!

BONUS

RETIREMENT
TOOL KIT

KEEP THIS HANDY
FOR
MOMENTS OF STRESS

Quick Relief For Times Of Stress

I need you darling, you complete me.

As an efficient manager of your life and home, you probably want tools that make you more organized and productive. The Retirement Tool Kit offers a quick reference to help you reflect on the joys of retirement marriage if you ever find yourself stressed over something you regretted happening.

Picture this scenario. You and your spouse have developed a plan for staying happily married. You've agreed on the activities you enjoy doing together and by yourselves. You appreciate one another's strengths and have developed a method for sharing tasks around the house. You are enjoying your retirement relationship

Even this perfect scenario can sometimes go awry, however. You or you mate forgets to be kind and considerate or finds it difficult to compromise on something that really matters to the other person.

This is when the Retirement Tool Kit can be put into action. It can help you reflect on your marriage and what really matters to you and your mate. It can inspire you to respond positively to whatever might have annoyed or shocked you in that particular moment.

As you read through the following reminders, you will find plenty of space to write notes to your-self on the pages and make those pages especially meaningful to you.

THE SEVEN TOOLS IN YOUR SURVIVAL KIT

One: Practice Gratitude

Taking time to identify something to be grateful for each day advances our ability to ignore petty annoyances. Reflecting on what's really important in life helps us reduce our inclination to harbor negative thoughts and to become more inclined to practice kindness.

You may choose to keep a daily journal of your gratitude thoughts—or you may simply decide to reflect on one idea each day. The important part of practicing gratitude is that you do just that – practice it! Every day take the time to find at least one thing you can be grateful for. It can be something simple, like not having to get up early for work or for the kids, or being able to hire someone to cut the lawn after all those years of doing it yourself.

Research has shown that "people who regularly practice gratitude by taking time to notice and reflect upon the things they're thankful for, experience more positive emotions, feel more alive, sleep better, express more compassion and kindness, and even have stronger immune systems. And gratitude doesn't need to be reserved only for momentous occasions."

Derrick Carpenter, MAPP, *The Science of Gratitude*

Two "Must Do's"
For A Successful Retirement Partnership

Communicate Regularly

If you don't tell your partner what makes you happy or sad, how will he or she know what is important to you? Revealing what you are thinking and feeling helps your spouse understand you better.

When you share a new discovery you have made, or events you have experienced each day, it makes you a more interesting partner; it often leads to stimulating conversations and common interests that may surprise you and enhance your relationship.

Forgive Easily

What's the point of holding a grudge? It makes you unhappy and creates an unpleasant atmosphere!

According to *Wikipedia*, Forgiveness is the intentional and voluntary process by which a person undergoes a change in feelings and attitude regarding an offense, lets go of negative emotions and increases one's ability to wish the offender well. This isn't always easy to do; like anything else, it takes practice. This is why the toolkit is here. Use it as a quick remainder of ways to nurture your relationship and foster a happy relationship in your marriage.

Three Practices To Remain Calm
In A Retirement Marriage

1. Be a little deaf sometimes.
Chief Justice Ruth Bader Ginsburg revealed this advice, given to her on her wedding day by her mother-in-law, as the best advice she ever received and the key to her long and happy marriage.

2. Practice empathy
Taking time to consider the feelings and emotions of our partners inspires us to seek understanding of our mate's actions or statements and strengthens our ability to com-promise and care for one another.

3. Maintain a positive attitude
Allowing ourselves to be negative about life typically leads to finding fault with most everything…especially our life partners.

Four Reasons To Consider Retirement A Time of Renewal

Retirement has its special rewards. When our career responsibilities wind down we are gifted with opportunities to:

1. Foster deeper relationships.
2. Understand what is truly important in life.
3. Develop skills we have long wished to acquire.
4. Create a more joyful and meaningful marriage partnership.

What you choose to do with these opportunities is up to you, and is a major factor in how you enjoy retirement.

Five Initial Problems Many Retirees Experience

1. Loss of purpose
2. Loss of routine
3. Loss of authority
4. Loss of colleagues
5. Boredom

As you help yourself or your partner move beyond these losses, you create a retirement marriage built on trust, empathy and caring for one another

Six Habits of Happily Married Retirees

1. Listen
Consider the feeling behind your mate's angry or frustrated statement. Understanding one another's pain moves us toward compromise.

2. Compromise
The expression, *it takes two to tango* isn't just for dancing. Just as partners in a Tango move together to create a lovely dance, retired couples that respect one another's needs create their own harmony.

3. Laugh
What's not to like about laughing? It's good for your health, reduces stress and, according to a few researchers, working facial muscles by smiling helps reduce wrinkles and other signs of aging.

4. Hug
The nurturing touch of a hug builds trust and a sense of safety. Hugs elevate moods and create happiness, and the energy exchange between couples when hugging encourages empathy and understanding.

5. Share
Don't expect your partner to know what bothers you or makes you happy. You must share this information if you want it to be understood.

6. Care
Those who truly care for their mates find that it's natural to listen, to compromise, to laugh and to hug the most important person in their life. Their mate's happiness becomes their happiness.

Seven Practices to Develop In Retirement

1. Remember, retirement is not for sissies!
Creating a satisfying retirement marriage requires the involvement, courage and determination of both partners.

2. Entertain your wildest dreams.
Dreams can be the groundwork for meaningful retirement planning. They encourage us to consider what we really need and want in this new stage of life. Even when a dream seems too expensive or difficult to achieve, it encourages creative planning, and couples frequently find that they are surprisingly achievable, perhaps in a less costly or ambitious way, but fulfilling nonetheless.

3. Take the time to listen to what your spouse is really saying.
Too often, we think we heard what the other person said or don't listen at all. Solid relationships take empathy that is achieved only when we feel the other person's pain, concerns or desires.

4. Identify what you enjoy doing together.
Meaningful activities that both partners enjoy reduce the strain of too much togetherness and increases a couple's pleasure in spending time together.

5. Find reasons to compliment one another.
Kindness is contagious. It's harder to remain angry when the other person is kind to you. Kindness helps deepen your bond as a couple and helps you grow in your love and appreciation for one another.

6. Eliminate never, you always and should from your vocabulary.
When these words are used in a heated discussion, the accused partner hears only the accusation, not why the speaker is upset. Hearing "You NEVER take out the garbage," makes someone feel defensive. He probably did take the garbage out in the past week or two. Hearing "You always spend too much money," negates all the time he or she was thrifty. It shuts down an open dialogue where you are both listening to one another.

7. Remember to laugh.

Laughter truly is the best medicine to reduce stress or disappointment and even anger.

A NOTE FROM THE AUTHOR

As a young teacher and later an arts program coordinator, I saw how most of us learn by example. Then, as a confused wife with a newly retired husband, I experienced this truth first hand. My interviews with wives whose husbands had already retired, reassured me that my husband Art and I were not alone in needing to adjust to this new relationship. I also realized that if they could adjust, we could too.

It took time and energy, but we learned by their example. It became clear to us that, with the right attitude and commitment, couples can bring harmony and joy to their relationship. It doesn't matter that your definition of joy may be different from mine or your neighbors'. What does matter is that you and your life-partner find joy's best definition for the two of you and work toward those goals each day.

After writing the first edition of *Survive Your Husband's Retirement*, I continued to learn even more about creating a happy retirement and felt a strong desire to share these ideas with retired, or soon to be retired couples, in this Second Edition.

We wish you great success in your new life stage, and I look forward to meeting you on Facebook, on Twitter or in a retirement workshop I will be giving near your home.

For more on retirement issues, visit:
www.surviveyourhusbandsretirement.com

Or to contact me at:
nora@surviveyourhusbandsretirement.com

THOUGHTS FOR STAYING
HAPPILY MARRIED IN RETIREMENT

Care for One Another

Compromise

Be Grateful

Love and Laugh Often

And Art's Favorite, "Yes Dear"

Art and Nora Hall

NOTES

NOTES

NOTES

NOTES

Made in the USA
Columbia, SC
01 March 2018